PLANNING TO STAY

The Design Center for American Urban Landscape is a
research unit within the College of Architecture and Landscape
Architecture of the University of Minnesota. The Design
Center's mission is to educate public and private decision mak-
ers, professionals and citizens about the value of design
as a strategic partner with economic and social concerns in
the development of communities.

Design Center for American Urban Landscape Team:
William R. Morrish, Director
Catherine R. Brown, Senior Fellow in Urban Design
Harrison Fraker, Dean, College of Architecture and Landscape
Architecture
Michael Robinson, Research Fellow in Urban Design

Susan Braun, Graduate Research Assistant
Mary deLaittre, Graduate Research Assistant
Tim Fuller, Graduate Research Assistant
Dan Peterson, Graduate Research Assistant
Valerie Schillberg, Graduate Research Assistant
Betsy Leverty, Senior Accountant
Carol Salmon, Principal Secretary

Professional Advisors to Project Team:
Tom Martinson, City Planning and Neighborhood Revitalization
Charlie Quimby, Communications and Technical Writing
R.T. Rybak, Neighborhood Business Revitalization Strategies
Judith Martin, Urban Studies and Twin Cities Neighborhoods
Kristen McDougall, Graphic Design and Concept Communication
William Fleissig, Community Building Strategies

PLANNING TO STAY

A COLLABORATIVE PROJECT

by William R. Morrish and Catherine R. Brown

with Michael Robinson, Charlie Quimby and Susan Braun

With a Foreword by Neal Peirce

MILKWEED

EDITIONS

Published 1994, 2000 by Milkweed Editions

Printed in the United States of America

04 03 02 01 00 5 4 3 2 1

Planning to Stay was funded by The McKnight Foundation, Cowles Media Foundation, and Target Foundation for Dayton's and Target Stores.

Library of Congress Cataloging-in-Publication Data

Morrish, William R., 1948–

   Planning to stay : learning to see the physical features of your neighborhood / William R. Morrish and Catherine R. Brown. — 1st ed.

      p.   cm.

   ISBN 1-57131-246-3 (alk. paper)

   1. City planning — United States — Citizen participation.   2. Neighborhood — United States — Evaluation.   3. Community development, Urban — United States — Citizen participation. I. Brown, Catherine R., 1950–   . II. Title.

   HT167.M674 1994

   307.1'2 — dc20

94-25402

CIP

This book is printed on acid-free paper.

FOREWORD

We Americans have forever been a restless lot. We started out to settle a continent and "conquer the wilderness." We have often left ghost towns in our wake. In our rush to the ever-expanding rings of suburbia, we have effectively discarded whole sections of great cities. Our national characteristics, wrote de Crevecoeur in his *Letters from an American Farmer* over two hundred years ago, embrace love of newness, freedom to move, and unfettered individualism.

Planning to Stay is a radical assertion of a polar opposite in our national character. It says Americans also have a big place in their hearts for place and tradition, for history, for rootedness. Some of our greatest joys, this book asserts, come from community—the people and places of neighborhoods we cherish.

And a neighborhood need not, one reads in these pages, succumb to the machinations of special interest groups, or indifferent city bureaucracies, or political deals. The people and merchants of a neighborhood can become masters of their own destiny; they can shape their own physical and economic and social environment. The sole prerequisite: a pledge to each other, "We're planning to stay."

The delight of this book is that it not only gives the whys of neighborhood preservation and planning. It also provides the hows—the step-by-step elements of the planning process to involve an entire neighborhood in comprehending its weaknesses, its special strengths, and then spelling out its future in the context of the greater city about it.

Powerful, neighborhood-empowering images spring from these pages. We must learn the "visual rhythm" of open spaces, houses, churches, public buildings. The phrase "public gardens" is to cover every asset from great parks to community gardens. "Community streets" must be for pedestrians and cyclists as well as automobiles. And then there's the "neighborhood niche"— the variety of store façades, flower and vegetable stands, café tables, and merchandise displays that define each neighborhood's unique marketplace ambience—the diametric opposite, of course, of national franchise outlets, their quick-stop parking designs and coast-to-coast identical signs.

National franchisers, subdivision developers, realtors urging us to "buy up and out" may find this book dangerous. But for Americans who value their existing and historic communities, who want to stand their ground and define their own world against the force of outside interests, this book is sensationally good news. Here, at last, is a rationale and game plan for the preservation and progress of their neighborhoods—and by extension, our cities and nation.

—Neal R. Peirce

PLANNING A NEIGHBORHOOD

COMMUNITY MEMBERSHIP AN

ABOUT THE FUTURE OF ONE

DENTS AND MERCHANTS CAN

NEIGHBORHOOD, PARTICIPA

DECLARATION ABOUT THEMS

STAY." PLANNING TO STAY II

TRANSFORMING EXPERIENCE

8

COVER NEW DIMENSIONS O

AND A GOOD CITIZEN. WHEN

STAY" BECOMES AN ACTIVE V

IS EMBRACED, TWO QUESTIO

1. WHAT IS IT ABOUT THIS I
2. WHAT COULD WE ADD TO
US HERE?

IS A PARTICIPATORY ACT OF

 AN EXPRESSION OF BELIEF

S COMMUNITY. BEFORE RESI-

 BEGIN PLANNING FOR THEIR

TS MUST MAKE A SINCERE

LVES: "WE'RE PLANNING TO

 A NEIGHBORHOOD CAN BE A

N WHICH PARTICIPANTS DIS-

 BEING A GOOD NEIGHBOR

OUPLED WITH PLANNING, "TO

RB. ONCE THIS ACTIVE ROLE

S NEED TO BE ADDRESSED:

ACE THAT DRAWS US HERE?

THIS PLACE THAT WILL KEEP

Planning is an act of community participation and an expression of belief in its future.

Planning to Stay

PLANNING TO STAY BEGAN AS A BOOK ABOUT NEIGHBORHOOD PLANNING. IT BECAME A BOOK ABOUT SEEING.

Before residents and merchants can begin planning for their neighborhood, they ought to ask two questions: What is it about this place that draws us here? What could we add to this place that will keep us here in the future? Seeking the answers together can be a delightful learning process for the participants—and the start of a transforming experience for the neighborhood.

The first section of *Planning to Stay* provides a framework to help you see anew where you live and make it meaningful to you. With this book as a guide, you can develop tools to discover the physical resources you have, analyze what you find, compare it with what you admire, and describe what you want. Once armed with this new knowledge and deeper awareness, you may be ready to declare, "We're planning to stay." Then you will be ready to start building the neighborhood you envision.

The latter part of the book provides a step-by-step outline for planning that centers on what you have learned. Planning a neighborhood is an act of community participation and an expression of belief in its future. In the process, participants can discover new dimensions of being a good neighbor and a good citizen. When coupled with planning, "to stay" becomes an active verb.

Neighborhood planning processes are under way in Minneapolis, St. Paul, and other metropolitan communities. There are efforts throughout the metro area to promote economic development, enhance human services, improve educational opportunities, assure safety, provide access to transportation, and preserve the physical quality of life. But how do all of these activities unite in the comprehensive and livable places we call neighborhoods?

The McKnight and Cowles Media Foundations, with additional support from the Target Foundation, funded a study by the Design Center for American Urban Landscape to address the physical questions of building Twin Cities neighborhoods. The focus of this study is to help residents make plans and manage change in their neighborhoods. We discovered that neighborhood groups could benefit from learning to analyze their existing physical resources and identify what issues and concerns they could most productively address.

With *Planning to Stay*, we have attempted to show how considering the places we live in might play a larger role in generating more choices and better decisions for our cities. While our approach is based upon examining the physical character of neighborhoods, physical solutions by themselves will not solve social and economic problems. But neither can healthy economic and social conditions be sustained without a supportive physical environment. As with any urban problem, the relationships are complex, and all three areas must be considered in concert.

This is the first in a series of publications on neighborhood planning and design issues. As part of a multiyear commitment by the Design Center to help communities build quality neighborhoods, future publications will explore urban design strategies as ways of addressing issues faced by groups that are planning to stay.

THIS HANDBOOK HELPS NEIGHBORHOOD GROUPS DESIGN SOLUTIONS THAT:

— Generate innovative and creative options.

— Fit into the community.

— Build upon the positive physical aspects of the place.

— Create a physical environment that supports economic and social programs.

— Are both functional and beautiful.

— Unite neighborhoods into a cohesive fabric of city neighborhoods.

14

A WORD ABOUT WORDS

We have deliberately used new language for this book, because we are trying to help people see familiar things in a different way. This vocabulary shift is meant to help you express some important ideas about your neighborhood more vividly and precisely, without resorting to technical terminology.

We have avoided using standard "land use" terms used in typical city planning documents or descriptions you may assume you already understand. These new words reflect both the quality of places found in Twin Cities neighborhoods as well as their functional role in the making of community.

For example, we have found that neighborhoods can be and have been defined in many ways: from something as ethereal as "a state of mind" to something as mundane as an "area within the lines" of a planning map. We use "neighborhood" to describe the basic social unit and physical building block of our cities. We use "neighborhood niche" instead of "business/ commercial district" to describe specific neighborhood marketplaces. "Public gardens" is used instead of "park system" to embrace public and private open spaces, including small gardens and large campuses, in addition to our extensive city parks and recreation systems. The language we have chosen for this book—and the concerns these names express—are specific to the Twin Cities. For example, what we call public gardens might be a typical southwestern city's "public oasis." The language you choose will express what is appropriate for your conditions.

Language is a form of power, because it reflects a particular view of the world. New words can give you new power. By having to learn your neighborhood language, developers and officials will also have to acknowledge your way of seeing your environment.

Planning helps envision the future while building upon the resources of the past.

INTRODUCTION

The Neighborhood Made Visible

NEIGHBORHOOD PLANNING IS PRIMARILY A PROCESS TO LEARN ABOUT WHERE YOU LIVE...HOW TO SHAPE IT FOR THE BETTER...AND HOW TO SUSTAIN IT FOR THE LONG TERM.

How do we become aware of neighborhood change? When we see the letter from the city council member or neighborhood group announcing another meeting about another neighborhood issue?

More attention-getting is the sudden physical appearance of a change that has been occurring gradually. For example, seeing a neighborhood business close its doors . . . or a crack house open its doors. Noticing when the house being built next door turns out to be a triplex . . . or watching the neighborhood kids stand at bus stops and realizing they hardly know each other because they all attend different schools. Why? What could we have done? What can we do now?

It may be hard to muster the energy to sit through an evening of inconclusive opinion-venting after a hard day at work. We know it's better to anticipate change than to react after it's too late. But having "input into the process" seems like a small reward when the process itself isn't any fun and when the conclusion will rest on some political deal. Or, we may indeed have the motivation to act, but we haven't found ways to translate our dissatisfaction into action that will do any good.

Some neighborhoods have effectively used planning and organizing methods to envision their own futures and build upon the positive resources of their neighborhood. By establishing their own agendas, they have shaped public policy development and capital investment in the community. And, they would tell you, they have made new friends, learned to recognize important features and relationships that create a neighborhood character, and gained a new pride in the place where they live.

WHY PLAN? PLANNING AS A POWER TOOL FOR NEIGHBORHOOD BUILDING

There are many reasons for neighbors to come together to make a plan. Planning is one of the ways that residents can become involved in making decisions about their futures. A neighborhood is a specific physical place with particular distinguishing features and amenities. But it is also a community of common interests and associations. Whether in the beginning those interests are aggressively pursued or only dimly recognized, the community can come together to develop:

—a common understanding of the neighborhood's defining features,

—a vision for the future,

—a clear set of policies, plans, and actions for shaping growth and enhancing the area's physical fabric,

—specific strategies to secure support for projects that will improve the community.

Traditionally, neighborhoods plan in two ways: proactively, to anticipate change and continually build on existing resources, or reactively, to respond to change as it occurs. To plan proactively, residents need to gather and organize information that outlines needs, supports opportunities, and identifies a range of options. The resulting focused agenda becomes the basis of neighborhood power. It enables residents to collaborate on a more equal footing with the private and public interests that traditionally have made the economic and political decisions that affect neighborhood life.

You can use the steps outlined here to help your neighborhood make proactive plans to guide future growth—to support, for example, the seeking of private investment or public funds, such as Minneapolis Neighborhood Revitalization Program funding. And you can use the same ideas to react to projects that may have an impact on your neighborhood—for example, establishing criteria for evaluating a new retail development or a proposed residential complex.

WE BELIEVE THAT:

— Downtowns symbolize cities. Neighborhoods define them.

— Working together, neighbors can make plans that shape the economic, social, and physical environment in which they live.

— Planning begins by identifying and defining the physical attributes and structure.

— And with the help of local government, neighborhoods can plan their own destinies in ways that respect the needs of adjacent neighborhoods and the city as a whole.

SEVEN OTHER REASONS TO PLAN

Once neighborhoods accept these "big reasons" and decide to plan, there are other reasons that a neighborhood plan makes sense:

LINKING NEIGHBORHOODS If neighborhoods have coherent plans developed in a common fashion, their mutual interests in broad public policy or major projects can be coordinated more effectively—with the kind of vision that makes livable neighborhoods into exceptional cities.

CONTRIBUTING TO COMPREHENSIVE CITY PLANS Neighborhoods are the building blocks of cities. With more than one hundred distinct neighborhoods in the Twin Cities, comprehensive city planning cannot possibly deal with the intensely local, block-by-block concerns. However, neighborhood plans can add up to a comprehensive mosaic when coordinated by effective municipal planning.

SHAPING AGENDAS BY COMMON INTERESTS VERSUS SPECIAL INTERESTS Community agendas driven by narrow interests can drive away participants. A process based upon the common interests of neighborhood residents may find a way to resolve issues without confrontative tactics or back-room dealmaking.

PROVIDING A FRAMEWORK FOR PUBLIC AND PRIVATE INVESTMENT DECISIONS Neighborhoods that have a clear agenda and development policies are more attractive to developers and investors. A solid neighborhood plan eliminates surprises and helps the developer design a project that truly meets the community's expectations. By articulating broad needs, the plan can reveal undiscovered investment opportunities.

GETTING A PLACE AT THE TABLE A neighborhood that plans for its future is applying the same principles as the public and private interests traditionally sitting at the table where development decisions are made. The neighborhood that can speak a similar language can better advocate its own interests.

DECIDING WHAT TO KEEP AND WHAT TO TEAR DOWN All neighborhoods age and change. As they progress through their normal maturation cycles, residents are constantly debating which economic, social, and physical attributes need to change and which should be kept. By identifying and understanding the basic services and important symbols of continuity, you can incorporate these stabilizing cornerstones in community development plans.

BUILDING A FOUNDATION TO ADDRESS BROADER SOCIAL AND ECONOMIC ISSUES Social and economic issues aren't political abstractions in neighborhoods. They show up in vacant buildings; untended lots; unsafe streets, schools, and playgrounds; and hostility among neighbors. By working on physical planning, your neighborhood will be working on broader issues, too.

BEFORE YOU DECIDE WHAT YOU NEED, KNOW WHAT YOU ALREADY HAVE. BEFORE YOU DECIDE WHAT WILL BE, KNOW WHAT MIGHT BE.

A FRAMEWORK
FOR DESCRIBING YOUR NEIGHBORHOOD

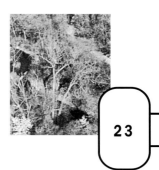

WE COMPREHEND WHERE WE LIVE BY SEEING, IDENTIFYING, AND CATEGORIZING THE PHYSICAL FEATURES THAT DEFINE OUR HOME, NEIGHBORHOOD, AND CITY.

Flying over the Twin Cities, we see a rich carpet of homes and gardens, organized in a grid of blocks stretching outward from the downtown, commercial spires of Minneapolis and St. Paul toward the northern lakes and southern farms.

On a city map, our neighborhoods appear as a pattern of squares and rectangles devoid of activity. This grid is interrupted and redirected by freeways, hills, lakes, and the Mississippi River. A planning map defines the boundaries of the one hundred colored patches named for parks, schools, and topographic features we call neighborhoods. And on television, the weather radar map dissolves all detail except the cold, heat, or humidity that will be ours for the next twenty-four hours.

These abstract maps meet a specific purpose but mask how variations in physical features give each neighborhood a unique identity. A railway lined with grain elevators cuts through one area. A creek meanders through another. The breeze carries the smell of the lake, or the Swedish bakery, or grilling kielbasa. Ornate streetlights seem scaled for nocturnal strollers instead of traffic. An elegant canopy of elms still survives here. There we notice ample front porches, sloping lawns, and flowering bushes.

These are some of the physical resources of the Twin Cities.

Identifying specific neighborhood resources can help us construct a more realistic image of the place where we live. Categorizing what we have becomes the foundation for plannning what to keep, what to add, and what to change. And seeing these resources as part of a larger, interdependent framework helps us reconcile the streetcar-defined neighborhoods from which our cities grew with the automobile-dependent metropolis we have created.

24

Physical features give each neighborhood a unique identity.

UNDERSTANDING THE FRAMEWORK

This section introduces a vocabulary of five physical features and five organizing themes. Taken together, these concepts provide a framework to help you comprehend the physical resources and the quality of your neighborhood by considering one element at a time.

Looking at each physical feature in light of the five organizing themes—as we do in the following pages—will suggest questions you can ask about your neighborhood. These questions will help you identify the important local characteristics of each physical feature and diagnose the issues that affect the quality of the neighborhood. They will also help you clarify the choices you can make that will shape your neighborhood now and in the future.

PHYSICAL FEATURES

Physical features are the tangible resources that express a neighborhood identity, influence its values, and shape its social and economic structures. We have chosen physical features that seem to be important in shaping Twin Cities neighborhoods: homes and gardens, community streets, neighborhood niches, anchoring institutions and public gardens.

HOMES AND GARDENS are the spaces where we rear our families, sustain our daily existences, display our identities, and contribute to the overall neighborhood image. We often share these spaces with friends and neighbors. The home and garden feature can be found in many types of housing units—from the single family house with lot to the multifamily unit with courtyards, patios, and balconies. In every home type, it is important to have a sense of privacy within the dwelling and yet be connected at will to the natural environment and the larger community.

COMMUNITY STREETS are lanes that supply a functional and pleasant balance between use by automobiles and pedestrians. These streets provide significant social spaces for sidewalk conversations, walking the dog, and strolling the baby. These informal activities can coexist with traffic when streets are scaled to pedestrian dimensions and proportions.

NEIGHBORHOOD NICHES are the places where neighbors purchase the basic goods and services—as well as some of the specialty items—that support their daily activities. Haircuts and hardware. Pizza and pastries. Pumping bicycle tires, renting movies, and picking out birthday cards. For all the gravitational pull of downtowns and malls, these service zones survive and contribute to the signature of a neighborhood.

ANCHORING INSTITUTIONS are the places where the cultural, educational and social traditions of our communities are centered. The elementary school, the parish church, the library, the community recreation center, and even the local brewery or auto plant help structure the social patterns and focus the community life of our neighborhoods.

PUBLIC GARDENS connect us individually and collectively to the natural environment. These public open spaces allow people of many ages, ethnic origins, and economic circumstances to gather together. At bandstands, ball diamonds, fishing docks, and vegetable gardens, we exercise the skills of acting in public, observing community norms, enjoying common pursuits, and just getting outdoors.

The quality, accessibility, and convenience of these features establish a neighborhood's image and character. How we maintain and build upon these physical resources determines its livability.

ORGANIZING THEMES

Five organizing themes provide a set of principles that enable us to evaluate the quality and relationships of a neighborhood's physical features according to location, scale, mix, time, and movement.

LOCATION is concerned with where a feature is placed in relation to our homes and other physical features as well as how it is situated on a particular site. Location is the starting point for asking questions about the quality, usefulness, and relationships of any neighborhood feature.

Decisions about placement collectively influence the image of a neighborhood. Some of these relationships are obvious, and regulations already exist to manage them, such as the appropriate distance between a liquor store and a school. But more often, the issues are subtle and concern how features enrich their immediate surroundings and connect the community to the larger context of the city. For example, the St. Paul Cathedral is an integral feature of its neighborhood, yet it is also a visible and treasured symbol for the whole city.

Physical orientation on a site influences how well a feature can support its intended use. Situation on the site also affects the uses of surrounding features. Take neighborhood churches, for example. Typically, the large congregation hall and tall spire are located forward on the site, creating a grand public entrance on the street. Classrooms and meeting spaces, closer in height to surrounding homes, are located to the side or rear.

SCALE has to do with the size of things and their proportion to other things within the same view. In neighborhoods particularly, matters of scale are determined in relation to our human proportions. Without knowing exactly why, we may sense that the store is too far, the building is too large, the street is too busy, the path is too narrow, or the playground is too small. These perceptions about scale can usually be expressed in actual dimensions related to surroundings. A sidewalk that measures four feet wide may be ample on a residential street but may seem severely cramped in a commercial area. A three-story brick home that seems visually appropriate in an older neighborhood will be incompatible amid postwar ramblers. We carry around an intuitive tape measure that allows us to judge whether physical features feel comfortable and appropriate. With a little probing, we can fine-tune our sense of scale. It might be as simple as taking an actual tape measure to a favorite space and measuring it. Or checking the width of a commercial sidewalk in proportion to the number of people walking and dining on it. Or testing how far we can walk in five minutes. Understanding why we find particular features appealing can help us see why specific buildings and spaces are successes or failures.

MIX is primarily concerned with sets of uses and activities that make a neighborhood livable for all residents. As neighborhoods change, adjusting the mix becomes critical. Do the people who live there find their needs met for transit, housing types, entertainment, recreational activities, essential goods and services? What uses exist today? What should be added? Where are they located, and how are they connected physically? Are the respective uses appropriate and mutually supportive? By providing the right mix for its residents, a neighborhood can sustain its vitality over time. By creating a special mix of features, such as ethnic restaurants, unique shops, neighborhood gardens, and seasonal festivals, a neighborhood can create a signature that differentiates it from others.

Neighborhoods can adapt to the changing needs of its residents.

TIME involves looking at how a neighborhood's physical structures support day and night routines, adapt to seasonal changes, and provide a sense of continuity. Time is particularly critical in the Twin Cities, with our cold climate and long periods of fewer daylight hours. During the winter, residents turn inward, coming outside only to shovel snow or pursue winter recreational activities. In summer months, people burst outdoors into yards and gardens, lakes, parks, and streets. Climate clearly influences the community spirit. Neighborhoods must plan activities and design physical structures from a perspective that takes into account four seasons plus nighttime uses.

Existing neighborhoods are largely a creation of decisions by past residents—from the choice of trees and building styles to the siting of parks and the configuration of street grids. Thus, planning groups inevitably must address considerations of history, memory, tradition, and culture as they exist in places and structures. How well we incorporate landmarks and adapt old spaces for contemporary uses will determine the quality of the neighborhood we pass to the next generation.

MOVEMENT considers accessibility to physical features within the neighborhood as well as to amenities within the larger metropolitan area. This theme addresses how we organize transportation between residential areas and the places we work, shop, and recreate. It recognizes the movement of pedestrians and bicycles as being integral, rather than subservient, to the needs of automobiles and public transit systems. Movement is concerned with designing clear, safe, and pleasant passageways necessary for daily living. A related concern is how we organize the features that are our destination so we reach them conveniently, without undue reliance on the automobile. Finally, what is the spatial quality of our movement system? How do neighborhood patterns fit into the citywide and metropolitan systems, while maintaining their desired local character?

By applying these five themes to what we see, we can more easily detect similarities, differences, and relationships among the resources in our various neighborhoods. These themes can help us describe our responses to particular physical features in more sophisticated ways. When we know why we like or dislike a particular feature, we can begin to discuss what to keep or change.

Homes and Gardens

HOMES AND GARDENS ARE THE SPACES WHERE WE REAR OUR FAMILIES, SUSTAIN OUR DAILY EXISTENCES, DISPLAY OUR IDENTITIES, AND CONTRIBUTE TO OUR NEIGHBORHOOD'S IMAGE.

The Twin Cities residential landscape is dominated by the single-family house and yard. For many people, this combination not only satisfies a basic housing need—it also symbolizes their hopes and achievements. Yet a freestanding, single-family house is not the only home. In every neighborhood, residents of varying ages, family situations, and income levels need a variety of home types. These include duplexes and fourplexes, units above retail spaces, and large apartment buildings with their porches, patios, balconies, and common gardens. As the age and economic demographics of a neighborhood change, the housing stock should also diversify so that residents can stay—throughout their lives, if they desire.

In the past, the home has filled a variety of needs. It has served as the family hearth, the center of work, education, health care, entertainment, child-rearing, and socializing. Today, many of those functions have shifted from our dwellings to institutions and commercial establishments, such as schools, hospitals, fast-food restaurants, child-care centers, and health clubs.

As a private domain, the home can be a place of peace and quiet enjoyment. It can also be isolated and lonely, without access to the institutions and services that enrich the basic functions of the home. Home is more than a shelter that is high, dry, warm, and secure. It is also a physical link to the larger community and the natural environment .

Visual connections reinforce feelings of safety.

LOCATION: *AMONG NEIGHBORS*

Our homes are located among neighbors: the families next door, the couple down the street, or the trusted merchant across the alley. These are the people we know or at least recognize as belonging. We may spend time in each other's homes or simply encounter each other while shoveling snow or strolling down the block. We look out for one another. People driving past or walking, biking, or visiting sense that they are among neighbors—and that they are expected to act as neighbors themselves. The sense of visual and social connections among us reinforces feelings of trust and safety.

YOUR SITE RELATIONSHIPS

How is your home set on its site? How far is the front of your building from the sidewalk and from your nearest neighbor?

From your house, yard, window, or balcony, do you have views of your block or any physical, neighborhood features, such as public gardens?

Do you have direct access or connections to outdoor space, sunlight, and air by way of decks, porches, balconies, gardens, or courtyards?

Are houses and buildings and gardens in your neighborhood placed to enhance the benefits and mitigate the negative impacts of natural forces, such as sun and wind? What kinds of improvements could be made?

YOUR BLOCK RELATIONSHIPS

Where is your home within the block? Is it on a corner or midblock? How does the location of houses and other features enhance or detract from your block?

Who lives next door? Across the street or alley? On the other blocks of your neighborhood?

Is your block on the edge of the neighborhood or near the center?

What kinds of goods, services, entertainment, educational opportunities, and jobs lie within a ten-minute walk from your home?

WHERE IS YOUR NEIGHBORHOOD IN THE CITY?

Is your neighborhood near downtown, clustered with other neighborhoods in the middle of the city, or positioned along the boundary with another community?

Is your neighborhood near a primary destination—an institution or physical feature used by people from all over town—such as the State Capitol, Lake Como, Lake of the Isles, or the airport?

What aspects of residential life are affected by your neighborhood's location?

Trees, gardens, and parks help homes fit together.

SCALE: *VISUAL RHYTHM*

In residential areas of the Twin Cities, the visual rhythm of buildings and open spaces sets familiar patterns. This rhythm varies among neighborhoods; each has its own dimensions. We feel comfortable when we sense that the proportion between open spaces and the mass of buildings is right for the neighborhood. Buildings that are inappropriately high and close together—reducing air movement, green space, or access to the sun—make us feel uneasy. They seem to be overrunning the natural environment. Yet a variety of home types—even medium-density, multifamily housing—can be located together without destroying the character of the block or the peace of the neighbors, if appropriate proximity is maintained.

BUILDING SIZE AND MASS

How long, tall, or deep are the typical, individual houses and other buildings on your block?

Do the dimensions of the buildings differ widely? How widely?

Which buildings seem to be appropriate in size and mass? Which are inappropriate? How might they be improved?

OPEN-SPACE PROPORTIONS

What are the typical dimensions of the front yards, side yards, and backyards of buildings on the block?

Which spaces are proportioned well to the buildings they separate? Which aren't?

How do physical elements such as trees, gardens, and porches help homes on the block fit together?

Are there unimproved, open spaces that could be improved to help the buildings fit together?

Integrate new spaces and reuse older ones.

MIX: *VARIOUS HOME TYPES*

Demographic changes in our cities alter the housing mix we need. Diversifying can mean adapting institutional and industrial buildings, creating apartments above retail spaces in neighborhood niches, improving existing housing, or rearranging housing units within blocks. Such changes raise concerns about density, open space, off-street parking, and the scale and form of buildings.

VARIETY

How many different types of housing make up your neighborhood?

What are the physical characteristics—age, style, and quality—of those homes?

DOMESTIC ELEMENTS

Identify elements—such as porches, balconies, bay windows, courtyards, and fences—that enrich the homes and gardens in your neighborhood.

How might homes without them be improved to refine the character of the neighborhood?

PRESERVATION AND REUSE

Do any homes and gardens on the block reflect the area's history?

Is preservation of these homes important to the neighborhood's sense of historical continuity?

Are there opportunities to renovate homes or adapt existing buildings for new homes?

Streets change when residents move outdoors in warm weather.

TIME: *CONVERTIBLE SPACES*

Seasonal changes in Minnesota affect the character of many residences. Some homes have porches, decks, and other convertible spaces that mediate between indoors and out. When the weather warms, these spaces are modified, and reading, cooking, and socializing move outdoors. Yards and public spaces blossom with planting and activity. We see more of our neighbors. Lighting, too, extends our time to enjoy the neighborhood. And the lighting of streets, yards, and porches allows us to be outside at night and makes us feel secure.

RESPONSE TO THE SEASONS

Which exterior features—windows, gardens, and porches—connect neighborhood homes or apartments to the natural environment?

How do residents modify them to accommodate seasonal activities?

LIGHTING

Do homes and apartment buildings in your neighborhood have exterior lighting for yards, parking areas, and doorways? Is the lighting used throughout the neighborhood, especially in winter?

Is street lighting intended for cars or pedestrians? Does it brighten paths or intersections? Does it make you feel safe or leave you wanting to dash past the shadows for home?

MOVEMENT: *STARTING POINT*

Home is where we start from. Once out the door, each of us quickly establishes a path to our daily destinations. We head into the corridor, down the elevator, and around the corner to the bus stop. Or across the neighbor's yard and through the park to school. Or out to the garage, down the alley, and into the street. The quality of these paths and the independence with which we can reach the city's amenities define our domestic landscapes. What we can freely experience outside our immediate neighborhoods influences the joy and enrichment we gain from living in our city.

COMING AND GOING

Do dwellings in your neighborhood have private entries?

Are the entries protected for safety? Is outdoor standing space sheltered from the elements?

Do fences, gates, low walls, front gardens, steps, and other transitional elements add character and visual interest to the block?

Do front porches, stoops, stairs, and ramps welcome visitors?

QUALITY OF PASSAGE

What is the condition of hallways, stairs, elevators, common areas, and front walks between your home and the street?

What affects the quality of transition spaces between the buildings on your block, and between the public street and the privacy of your home?

How is the quality of your paths affected by lighting; trees and plants; the condition of buildings, sidewalks, and streets; and the activities you encounter?

Do neighboring windows, doors, and lighting make you feel safe when passing between your home and a parking area or bus stop?

EASE OF MOVEMENT

Do metropolitan transit systems connect the people in your home to a variety of goods, services, and work places?

Are food, recreation, and other amenities available within a ten-minute walk?

Community Streets

COMMUNITY STREETS ARE PUBLIC RIGHTS-OF-WAY, WHICH UNITE NEIGHBORHOODS, PROVIDE ACCESS FOR MOTORISTS AND NONMOTORISTS, AND PROMOTE NEIGHBORHOOD IDENTITY, HEALTH, COMFORT, AND SAFETY.

Because streets claim thirty percent of the land around our homes and neighborhoods, they are too dominant a physical feature to be used simply for moving vehicles and people. Streets can also become community spaces that connect homes and bind neighborhoods into cities.

Our mental maps of the city are based on familiar street grids. We see the street skeleton before we perceive the substance of the neighborhoods that lies within it. True, streets mark the outlines of city blocks and the locations of individual properties, but the attributes of those properties color the quality and identity of the streets. For example, Summit Avenue's appeal is not its pavement. The street is an extended outdoor space defined by wide, planted boulevards and a procession of stately homes and institutions. The Russian word for avenue—*prospekt*—captures this sense of such an outdoor room with a view.

Think of streets as neighborhood hallways. Like the hallways in a home, streets are three-dimensional rooms with their own characters. Each character is shaped by the styles and heights of buildings, by tree canopies, fences, hedges, porches, lawn sizes, lighting styles, and the spaces between buildings. Each street arouses a different pitch of feeling. When you move along a community street, you know that you are in someone's neighborhood and not just on a thoroughfare.

Streets move traffic, but they also host a range of social and commercial activities. Neighborhoods are enhanced and drivers enjoy the scenic route where the streets are made for walking. And streets build community when they unify neighborhoods and transport people safely and conveniently.

The community street connects us to the city and to one another.

LOCATION: *BEYOND THE FRONT DOOR*

Visually, the street begins just outside the front doors of homes, stores, and offices. Its impact comes from more than just the look of the roadway, sidewalk, and boulevard. The street is also defined by the parks, commercial areas, institutions, and front yards along it. It formally connects residents, creates a sweep of lawns and gardens, and provides the first common space for informal neighborhood encounters. The community street begins our connection to the rest of the city.

COMMUNITY STREETS AS CONNECTORS

Which are your most important neighborhood streets? What makes them important?

Which streets in your neighborhood primarily serve people passing through? Which serve local uses?

How do these streets link neighbors or connect residents to the neighborhood's anchoring institutions and neighborhood niches? To other neighborhoods and the larger community?

Do public transportation services connect you adequately to other neighborhoods, the downtown area, and the larger community?

Do your neighbors keep up their sidewalks and alleys? Can neighbors casually gather there?

COMMUNITY STREETS AS BOUNDARIES

Which streets mark your neighborhood's borders?

Do you think of these boundary streets as parts of your neighborhood?

Which other neighborhoods share these streets?

SCALE: NEIGHBORHOOD PROPORTIONS

A community street is scaled in proportion to the nearby homes and gardens, neighborhood niches, anchoring institutions, and public gardens. It is also scaled to suit the pedestrians, bicyclists, and transit riders who share it with motorists. The proper width of sidewalks and streets depends on building height and on the type and density of activity. Sidewalks and roadways that fit neighborhood proportions create a unified, livable environment. And they still serve both the pedestrian and the driver.

     In other words, streets have purposes beyond moving traffic, and streets and sidewalks come in more than one width.

SIDEWALK AND STREET RELATIONSHIPS

Are your neighborhood's sidewalks and road-ways sized primarily to suit the needs of automotive traffic? Or does their scale equally accommodate pedestrian activity?

Do building facades enhance sidewalk activity?

Are pedestrians buffered from vehicle traffic by generous sidewalks, parallel-parking strips, or other physical elements?

Are parking lots set back from the streets and separated by sidewalks?

PEDESTRIAN RELATIONSHIPS

How many pedestrians use the street? Do their activities vary with time or place? Is the side-walk wide enough to handle them comfortably?

Are street elements—such as sidewalks, light-ing, and trees—scaled to pedestrian dimensions?

Street vitality depends on the activities that occur on both sides of the curb.

MIX: *FUNCTIONAL BALANCE*

A community street strikes a balance between motorist and nonmotorist. Life on the street occurs on both sides of the curb: driving, parking, walking, biking, raking leaves, washing cars, playing street games, and other socializing. Neighborhood niche activities, such as outdoor dining and sidewalk sales, also confirm the street as true community space. The alley, too, is an important neighborhood area with a dual role—as a service space for parking, loading, and garbage collection, and as a footpath.

BALANCE OF VEHICLE AND PEDESTRIAN USES

How are streets and alleys used in your neighborhood? Do these uses reflect the needs and desires of residents and business owners?

How do your streets balance vehicle uses (by autos, delivery trucks, public transit, and bicycles) and pedestrian uses (including baby strollers, shopping carts, and wheelchairs)?

Are transit stops adequate, convenient, safe, and comfortable? Do buses provide links to the neighborhood's prominent features—neighborhood niches, public gardens, and anchoring institutions?

Which features—such as parking bays, off-street parking, sidewalk displays, bus stops, benches, and cafés—encourage vehicles and pedestrians to mingle?

BALANCE OF SERVICE AND PUBLIC SPACES

Could commercial and recreational activities coexist in spaces such as alleys and parking areas? Could businesses with staggered periods of peak activity share off-street parking?

Are service spaces in your neighborhood buffered from public and residential areas by plantings, fences, landscaped open spaces, or other devices?

Seasonal changes affect the activities in your neighborhood.

TIME: DAY/NIGHT ACTIVITIES

Streets can be busy with many pedestrian activities throughout the day and evening. Those activities can begin, for example, with early morning markets and extend through the evening with sidewalk dining and strolling. A pedestrian-friendly environment features lighting that promotes safety, enhances comfort, and extends activities into the evening.

Vehicles and pedestrians can share the same streets.

TIME-OF-DAY AND SEASONAL CHANGES IN ACTIVITIES

Do your community streets support a variety of daytime activities? How could your neighborhood extend the hours when its streets seem safe and welcoming?

How do seasonal changes in street activity affect the sense of safety?

Do seasonal celebrations in your neighborhood temporarily take over the streets? If not, where could such celebrations be started?

How does weather—particularly snow and its removal—affect street activities?

Are the passages to bus stops adequately lit for early morning and evening riders—especially in winter?

TIME-SHARING SPACE

Could pedestrians and vehicles use the same space at different times, on different days, or in different seasons?

How would management, lighting, or other systems have to be changed to permit this kind of time-sharing?

Leafy vistas make community streets inviting to pedestrians and motorists alike.

MOVEMENT: *ENHANCED PASSAGE*

Every driver is sometimes a pedestrian, but most people like to be welcomed no matter how they're traveling. We city dwellers take our Sunday drives where people like to walk: along parkways, boulevards, and leafy, residential lanes. These pedestrian-oriented streets enhance our comfort and safety with boulevard trees, wide sidewalks, planted medians, and ample lighting and crosswalks. The same features that enhance walking also make the street pleasant for driving.

FROM A PEDESTRIAN POINT OF VIEW

Do trees, pedestrian-scale lighting, and street furniture claim your street for pedestrians? How does this orientation signal "neighborhood" to people passing through?

How could the views and curbside structures along your streets be redesigned for the enjoyment of pedestrians and motorists alike?

What kinds of vistas, geographic features, and street arrangements can beautify a street?

At intersections in your neighborhood, do curb ramps, widened sidewalks, and other improvements increase accessibility, protect pedestrians, and ease congestion?

RETHINKING PATTERNS AND HABITS

How much traffic travels on your community streets? How much of that traffic is created by neighborhood residents?

What are your neighborhood traffic patterns? Could people consolidate trips or walk to reduce traffic congestion? What would encourage residents to change their traffic habits?

How could you reduce traffic by changing the way you use your vehicle?

Does traffic in your neighborhood regularly exceed posted speed limits?

MOVEMENT TO, FROM, AND ALONG TRANSIT ROUTES

Is the passage from your home to the transit stop pleasant, safe, and comfortable?

Is the transit stop well lit and well maintained? Are seats provided?

Is the stop protected from inclement weather?

Do transit vehicles stop near centers of neighborhood activity, such as parks, commercial areas, schools, and entertainment centers?

Neighborhood Niches

NEIGHBORHOOD NICHES ARE THE MARKETPLACES WHERE NEIGHBORS FIND THE BASIC GOODS AND SERVICES—AS WELL AS SOME OF THE SOCIAL ENCOUNTERS—THAT ENRICH THEIR DAILY LIVES.

"Neighborhood niche" is not just a fancy term for "commercial district." We use that phrase to emphasize the special relationship between a residential area and the nearby businesses that serve as focal points for the neighborhood. A neighborhood niche might be one establishment, a commercial crossroads, or a section of an extended district. Niche businesses are owned by valued members of the community, who attend to minor emergencies, promote community events, and make sure that the sidewalks are safe and clean. Their inventories of goods and services directly reflect neighborhood needs.

Niche shops sit tight against the sidewalks in buildings that often reflect the historic character of the neighborhood. Neighbors socialize on the sidewalks and in the doorways. The store facades can seem to enclose the street, turning it into an outdoor community room, furnished with merchandise displays, flower and vegetable stands, cafe tables, reader boards, and newspaper racks. No two neighborhood niches are alike.

These authentic, local marketplaces began to change as the automobile gained popularity and hyperextended the scale of our cities. Franchises appeared, armed with market research instead of knowledge about neighborhoods. They brought corporate managers, standard product lines, and formula buildings. Franchises need access by automobiles, high visibility, and quick-stop parking. To get these, many franchise retailers pull their buildings back from the curbs and build parking in front. This physical erosion of street corners contributes to the appearance of a purely automobile-oriented environment. Franchises are about the identical; neighborhood niches are about identity. Franchise rows look and act the same everywhere in America. Neighborhood niches are landmarks that identify particular locations in particular cities. As urban neighborhoods work to establish more livable environments, they may need to restore more balanced commercial patterns.

Neighborhood niches are commercial centers as well as outdoor community rooms.

LOCATION: *ON THE CORNER*

The storefronts in a neighborhood niche anchor the street corner and hug the sidewalk. The straight edge of their street walls encloses pedestrians and keeps the entire street scene in plain view, enhancing a sense of safety. Side and back parking lots act as service areas, and many are shared. The neighborhood niche's activity, local character, and prominent location make it a point of orientation for drivers and pedestrians.

CONCENTRATED ACTIVITY

Is there a center of commercial, social, and service activities in your neighborhood?

Does this area primarily serve the immediate neighborhood?

Does this area provide services that meet your varied needs on the weekends as well as more basic needs during the week?

Does the location of the buildings and parking areas define clear pedestrian pathways, street crossings, and activity zones?

Is there continuity in the outdoor space, or is it broken by large parking lots?

VISIBILITY AND SAFETY

Which features of the location orient people to the neighborhood?

Do any businesses or buildings convey local character and mark the niche as an interesting and unusual place?

Does street activity make the niche especially visible to passing drivers?

Do elements such as sidewalk dining and display windows add visual interest for motorists and pedestrians?

Do windowed storefronts face the street, helping pedestrians feel safe?

Are pedestrian paths clearly marked and heavily used, or must walkers pick their way through parking lots and unlit alleys?

Does curbside parking heighten convenience and buffer pedestrians from automobile traffic?

Streets and storefronts should invite pedestrians to linger.

SCALE: *PEDESTRIAN PROPORTION*

Whether it's one shop or a shopping district, a neighborhood niche reflects the scale of the homes around it. Its basic unit is a two- or three-story building with individual storefronts and street-level, owner-occupied businesses. Color, pattern, building materials, signage, awnings, and display windows are scaled to attract browsing pedestrians as well as passing motorists.

WELCOMING WALKERS

Do displays and windows of ground-floor shops in your neighborhood niche encourage browsing?

Do display windows, recessed doors, planters, arcades, and awnings act as transition zones between the street and the shops?

Do sidewalks provide enough space for retailers to extend their activities toward the street?

Is foot traffic encouraged by sidewalk lighting, plantings, furniture, or outdoor cafés and retailing?

Do setbacks in the street facade harbor seating, outdoor displays, or social activity?

Do canopies, awnings, or recessed doors shelter walkers and add color to the street?

Are service areas screened from nearby residences and public areas?

Neighborhood niches celebrate the diversity of communities.

MIX: *LOCAL MENU*

The niche provides goods, services, and jobs that serve the neighborhood residents, and its look underscores the community's identity. Individual storefronts with a variety of signs, forms, colors, and materials make a statement about the surrounding neighborhood's diversity. The local flavor of this mix may also draw people from other areas.

PHYSICAL AND CULTURAL MIX

What does the mix of storefronts in your neighborhood niche say about the people who live nearby? Is this a true reflection of the area's cultural diversity?

Do the storefronts and signs convey a sense of physical unity? Which elements of the street-facing wall add to or detract from this impression?

Do retail uses of the sidewalk enhance a feeling of safety? Do the public spaces promote social interaction?

UPSTAIRS/DOWNSTAIRS

Are the ground-level storefronts an attractive mix of retail, entertainment, and food-related facilities?

Does the ground-level mix carry over into an upstairs level of residential, retail, office, and service space?

Which activities might be moved upstairs or downstairs to add to the street's vitality?

MIX OF GOODS, SERVICES, AND JOBS

Does your niche provide the goods and services needed by its neighbors? By the larger community? Ask your neighbors which retail activities are missing.

Do your niche businesses provide jobs for community residents? Ask city planners about programs that would support start-up businesses in your neighborhood.

Could small-scale assembly plants or clean manufacturing be housed in your neighborhood niche? How about a community center?

Ask store owners which activities they would bring in to expand and stabilize their market.

TIME: SEASONAL MARKETS

Farmers' markets, annual street fairs, holiday lighting displays, outdoor cafés with extended hours, buildings from the streetcar era—such elements of neighborhood niches reflect daily, seasonal, and historic changes in neighborhoods. Extended evening hours make neighborhoods feel safer. Seasonal activities add opportunities for gatherings. And preserved buildings reinforce the identity of the niche and the history of the community.

SEASONAL AND OUTDOOR ACTIVITIES

Do businesses in your neighborhood niche extend their hours or expand outdoors during warmer months? How do these changes affect the vitality and liveliness of the street scene?

Which enterprises stay open in the evenings and on weekends? Is the neighborhood niche appropriately lit at night or for seasonal events?

Do these adjustments increase the use and safety of your neighborhood niche?

HISTORIC PRESERVATION

Which structures—particularly pre-automobile commercial and industrial buildings—add visual character and interest to the niche?

How might these structures be adapted to commercial uses while preserving their historic character?

Controlling auto congestion in your neighborhood niche creates a street-friendly environment.

MOVEMENT: *JUST DOWN THE STREET*

The neighborhood niche is the commercial equivalent of your next-door neighbor. It is just down the street from your home—or seems so, because you can reach it easily and safely by foot or bicycle. Because it is linked to the neighborhood by streets, the niche doesn't neglect the automobile either. Rather, it buffers pedestrians from cars and eases the transition to residential areas.

NEIGHBORHOOD ACCESS

Are passages between your neighborhood and niche safe and pleasant? Is the niche accessible from all directions?

Are sidewalks sufficiently wide to insulate pedestrians from auto traffic?

Are single-family homes separated from commercial buildings by parking, apartment buildings, landscaped open space, or other intermediate buffers?

PEDESTRIAN ACCESS TO THE NICHE

Are curbs sloped and buildings accessible to the elderly and people with disabilities?

Could transit stops be located midblock, allowing sidewalks to be widened and crosswalks to be shortened at intersections?

Are pedestrian crosswalks clearly marked?

Can the activities of your niche be linked other than at the street front? Do walkways through the block extend the auto-free environment?

Do sidewalk textures, lighting, and landscaping enhance the comfort and safety of the through-block connections?

Can the niche be linked to your neighborhood's public gardens or anchoring institutions?

PARKING AND TRANSIT

Can adequate parking be provided to the side or rear of commercial buildings so that retail activities can be clearly seen along the street?

Would some curbside parking buffer pedestrians from heavy traffic?

Would through-block connections to shared-parking areas promote activity within the block and reroute traditional pedestrian paths?

How well do buses connect the niche to the broader community?

Are the bus stops screened from traffic, lit well, accessible to all, and free from snow?

Anchoring Institutions

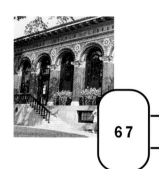

ANCHORING INSTITUTIONS ARE THE PLACES WHERE THE CULTURAL, EDUCATIONAL, AND SOCIAL ACTIVITIES OF OUR COMMUNITIES ARE FOCUSED.

In earlier times, neighborhood institutions often expressed their communities' social patterns and cultural values—and even shaped them. Parish churches were the focus of neighborhood activity, and elementary schools lent their names to their surrounding areas. Even as neighborhoods changed and residents had less in common, these anchoring institutions stayed. Their continuing presence helped preserve cohesive neighborhoods.

Not all anchors are religious, governmental, or educational institutions. And a neighborhood may have more than one anchor. In addition to schools, libraries, churches, synagogues, and fraternal lodges, anchors may include ethnic delis, food cooperatives, and significant employers. A park bandshell, fire station, or distinctive water tower might also express neighborhood identity. The essence of an anchor is that it answers community needs, serves a variety of social functions, and is structurally prominent without necessarily being monumental.

These institutions—with their spires, chimneys, domes, and water towers—give the neighborhood its skyline. The neighborhood might take its name from the institution—as do Seward, Cathedral Hill, Powderhorn Park, and Macalester. The anchor might serve as a focal point for the neighborhood—as do Sumner Library, St. Agnes Church, North High, and Cosetta's. Or it could be a signature institution—recognized well beyond the neighborhood: Mt. Olivet Church, the Schmidt Brewery, and the state fairgrounds. Some of these institutions serve only neighborhood residents, while others draw from the larger community.

Historic, ethnic, or aesthetic significance often colors the anchor's appearance. The physical form of the institution recalls its original role and reminds people of the neighborhood's cultural heritage. The landmark conveys a sense of permanence and continuity.

Anchoring institutions are prominent community signatures.

LOCATION: *PROMINENT SETTING*

Which came first—the anchoring institution or its prominent setting? Many institutions are found at key historic or geographic sites or at prominent addresses that heighten the institution's standing in the neighborhood. On the other hand, a clustering of institutions can create a prestigious location. And, in a few areas, such as the Guthrie-Walker-Loring Park area and the Capitol-Cathedral Hill axis, the combination of powerful institutions and powerful settings can imprint a cultural identity on a neighborhood or an entire city.

VISUAL PROMINENCE

Where are your anchoring institutions? What are their visual signatures?

How does location heighten the importance of their roles?

If an institution sits at a street-grid shift, major intersection, or other visually prominent site, how does its location emphasize its role as an anchor?

Have any institutions gained prominence by their nearness to other institutions?

GEOGRAPHIC PROMINENCE

Many anchoring institutions in the city occupy prominent geographical settings. How is an institution's importance communicated by its location on a hill, for example, or next to a body of water?

Do your neighborhood institutions occupy sites of historic events or significant settlements?

Do any sacred sites or important memorials in the neighborhood act as anchors, reinforcing neighborhood identity?

Anchoring institutions can use scale, architectural style, and building materials to respect surrounding neighborhoods.

SCALE: *FIT AND CONTRAST*

An anchoring institution that's properly proportioned and situated fits into its neighborhood, while any remarkable element distinguishes it as a landmark. The institution fits its context if its building and site are scaled to neighboring structures and open spaces. On the other hand, if the institution introduces a contrasting element—such as a church spire, a school theater, or civic plaza—the notable feature helps to identify the neighborhood.

IN PROPORTION TO THE NEIGHBORHOOD

Do your anchoring institutions seem to fit into the neighborhood?

Do elements such as lawns, wide sidewalks, building materials, side yards, and courtyards help fit the anchoring institution into its context?

Even though monumental in scale and institutional in form, does the anchor fit the architectural character of your neighborhood? Or does it look plunked down by an alien civilization?

OUT OF THE ORDINARY

Does a vertical element, such as a church steeple, set off the institution?

If the anchor relies on its overall size for its prominence, does it still reflect the proportions of neighborhood homes?

Does the contrasting element stand out so clearly that it's readily identifiable in the neighborhood? Is it visible and recognized outside the neighbohood, such as in the skyline?

Anchoring institutions, from art museums to social centers, can change to serve many community needs.

MIX: *SHARED SPACES*

As anchoring institutions change to meet their communities' needs, they also change physically. Moving from a single mission to multiple functions, for example, can demand architectural renovation—inside and out. Many churches have added playgrounds and day-care centers. A small, commercial building might be remodeled to house a center for teens or senior citizens.

PHYSICAL INTEGRATION

Which anchoring institutions serve multiple functions as, for example, churches, schools, day-care centers, playgrounds, and recreation halls?

Does the external arrangement of each building or mix of separate buildings reflect the variety of services? Do internal spaces reflect these uses?

Do those institutions use nontraditional spaces—such as commercial and residential buildings—to meet their expanded needs?

Do these institutions seem more physically integrated into the community by their transitional uses of buildings and spaces?

PROGRAM INTEGRATION

Which anchoring institutions serve as meeting places in your community?

Which of these are formal institutions, such as community centers, libraries, schools, and churches? Are there also informal centers, such as restaurants or stores?

Which social, cultural, educational, religious and political networks are fostered by neighborhood anchoring institutions?

Where do these networks intersect to enrich and integrate neighborhood life? For example, a park building might host Cub Scouts, a crafts class, a volleyball league, and a neighborhood planning meeting on the same evening.

Which anchoring functions are lacking in your neighborhood? Might existing institutions expand their services to bring more neighborhood residents together?

How do landmarks or seasonal celebrations reflect your neighborhood's ethnic or cultural history?

TIME: *TRADITIONS*

Neighbors eventually come and go, but anchoring institutions remain to bring permanence, stability, and continuity to the community. "Others have lived here before you and left us as their memorials," these institutions seem to say.

Institutions are important for the traditions they carry on as well as for the services they deliver. They recall the neighborhood's history and perpetuate familiar patterns of activity and seasonal celebration. Conversely, the loss or erosion of a school, church, fire station, or post office threatens a neighborhood's sense of continuity and tradition.

ACKNOWLEDGING AREA HISTORY

Which institutions reflect or acknowledge the area's history?

Which features of the institution express or support the neighborhood's traditions?

ANCHORING CELEBRATIONS

Which seasonal celebrations and activities are sponsored by anchoring institutions in your neighborhood? These activities may include not only highly visible cultural fairs and festivals, but also scouting, food drives, neighborhood athletic leagues, spring cleanups, Memorial Day ceremonies, or other events.

How do these events use theme, location, promotion, and participation to involve residents?

What signs of these celebrations or activities are visible in your community? How do they link the anchors to the neighborhood?

Do the celebrations reflect ethnic or cultural heritage and neighborhood history? Do they respond to changes in the seasons or time of day? Do they relate to citywide or worldwide celebrations?

Which seasonal events, celebrations, or festivals are held in nontraditional spaces, such as community streets or neighborhood parks?

MOVEMENT: ORIENTATION

Many anchoring institutions occupy high-visibility locations and are distinguished by prominent architectural elements that can be seen at a distance. Many people orient themselves by these landmarks. Historic brick breweries, graceful steeples, and ornate water towers mark visible and significant destinations in the neighborhood.

Anchoring institutions can also serve as mental landmarks. Cemeteries, corner coffee shops, libraries, and other landmarks remind us of the community's social, cultural, and historical roots.

ORIENTING LANDMARKS

Which features of anchoring institutions serve as orienting landmarks in your neighborhood?

Can prominent features also be seen from beyond the neighborhood? Are they visible from many points in nearby neighborhoods? Do visitors use them to find your neighborhood?

SIGNIFICANT DESTINATIONS

Which anchoring institutions are home to neighborhood and community gatherings?

Are these significant anchoring institutions visually and physically connected to public transit and vehicular, pedestrian, and bicycle routes?

SIGNATURE LANDMARKS

Which anchoring institutions symbolize and reflect the image of your neighborhood?

What is special about these institutions? For example, the College of St. Catherine is both the park and cultural focus for its neighborhood.

Public Gardens

PUBLIC GARDENS CONNECT US TO THE NATURAL ENVIRONMENT AND TO ONE ANOTHER.

Visionary planning of the Minneapolis and St. Paul parks systems at the turn of the century began the great legacy of open space in the metropolitan area. But the concept of the public garden represents more than the formal necklace of lakes, parks, playgrounds, and grand boulevards that encircles the cities. It also includes neighborhood jewels—pocket parks, community gardens, and public commons. And it includes unmanicured, natural systems, wetlands, abandoned rights-of-way, and other public lands.

Many public gardens are enriched with natural features—rivers, lakes, bluffs, hills, vistas, arbors, and greenery. Or they may offer constructed features, such as playgrounds, pools, courts, picnic grounds, pavilions, sculptures, and monuments. This public open space proclaims the compatibility of nature and city life and of diverse people with diverse interests. Residents may pursue their varied interests in active, organized recreation at hockey rinks, soccer fields, and ball diamonds. They may share open spaces with others who fish, Rollerblade, or grow vegetables. Or they can enjoy solitary contemplation of sails across a lake, daffodils along a path, or water splashing and swings creaking in the tot lot.

Public gardens can anchor a neighborhood's identity. Prospect Park is marked by a conical hill and historic water tower. Highland Park gazes down from its bluff onto a bend in the Mississippi River. Public open spaces are antidotes to density and important complements to private homes and gardens. The livability of cities hinges on places that welcome residents to come together with nature and each other. Collectively these features can become a city's signature. "The City of Lakes" refers to more than water. Minneapolis's public gardens and the access to its appealing natural features shaped the city's identity.

Our public gardens make our cities livable.

LOCATION: *ON COMMON GROUND*

Although streets might define our neighborhood borders, the public garden can form its center. Neighbors meet on a safe and equal footing in such a place. At the basketball court or flower garden, faces from beyond our block become familiar as we regularly meet those who share our routines and enjoyments, as well as common ground.

COMMON OWNERSHIP AND ACCESS

Does your public garden lie entirely inside your neighborhood, giving the residents a vested interest in maintaining and watching over it?

If the garden lies between neighborhoods, does its location separate or unify the communities that border it?

Are most residences within a five-minute walk of a public garden? Can children get there unchaperoned?

Is your park used only by neighborhood residents or also by people from elsewhere in the city? Why?

NATURAL ELEMENTS

Does your neighborhood have unusual topographical features that could be revealed by the creation of a public open space?

Could underlying geological or hydrological features be unearthed to enhance the built forms of your public gardens?

Which natural features and elements should be made more visible? How could they be preserved? Do they express neighborhood identity?

MAKING GARDENS FROM LEFTOVERS

If your neighborhood needs more public gardens, can you reclaim unused land?

Could alleys, cul de sacs, leftover parcels, or vacant lots be maintained as parts of your community's public gardens? Could they be transformed into flower gardens, tot lots, or vegetable gardens?

Public gardens can be designed to be a safe and beautiful part of your neighborhood.

SCALE: *VISUALLY ACCESSIBLE*

The size and visual accessibility of a neighborhood public garden are important. If you can see into and through a park, you will feel safe entering it. And, when an open space is visually linked to the surrounding neighborhood, it becomes a center of activity. People stop to watch, rest, or chat.

VISIBILITY FROM THE PERIMETER

Can you see through your park?

Does the placement of nearby housing permit neighbors to keep an eye on the open space?

SAFETY AND SECURITY

Does the organization of activity areas in your park make people feel safe and secure?

Can they see from one activity area into the others?

Are pathways and play areas well lit and well marked?

MIX: COMPATIBLE ACTIVITIES

Public gardens can host many activities. Spaces such as tennis and basketball courts, ball fields, and skating rinks support group sports. Pools, playgrounds, and fishing docks foster more informal, individual recreation. Benches, gardens, and paths encourage passive pursuits—people-watching, contemplation, strolling. Paths for bicycling and skating create a sense of energy and flow while connecting the neighborhood's public gardens to larger trail systems.

COMPATIBILITY WITHIN THE PARK

Do features of the public garden meet your neighbors' recreational needs? Or are jungle gyms, swings, and wading pools going unused while retired apartment dwellers miss their flower gardens?

Do the programs of the larger parks meet the recreational needs of the community? Do those programs and facilities reflect the interests of diverse ages and cultures?

Were buildings designed to blend with the landscape?

COMPATIBILITY WITH OTHER USES

Would a public garden reduce the density of buildings in the neighborhood?

Would a public garden allow greater density in nearby commercial or residential areas?

How do nearby homes or businesses help identify your public garden as a gathering place? Do they face the park or turn their backs on it?

How do adjacent spaces complement or detract from the open space? Can your open space help mediate between different or incompatible land uses?

Does a public garden lie next to a neighborhood niche or institution? Is it used for cultural events and community celebrations?

ACTIVE AND PASSIVE USES

Does your public garden support active and passive uses?

Do play areas and equipment support organized and informal recreation?

Are the spaces for active and passive activities appropriately placed? For example, do benches overlook the playground? Do flower gardens or bicycle paths give the play area a wide berth?

Is the open space suited to informal socializing? Are benches and sheltered areas provided to encourage people to pause and visit?

Our public gardens are outdoor clocks, which mark the seasonal passage of time.

TIME: *YEAR-ROUND ACTIVITIES*

As seasons change, so do Minnesotans' recreational activities. The outfield used in spring becomes a soccer field in the fall and a hockey rink in the winter. In summer, equipment moves out of the recreation center to support outdoor activities. Come winter, sailors return to the lakes to ice skate and swimmers to ski. Water and plants, too, are transformed by the seasons, and our public gardens show us these changes.

CHANGES IN FACILITIES AND PROGRAMS

Do changes in programming encourage year-round use of your public garden?

Are facilities designed to support activities for each season? Do building hours reflect seasonal changes in needs?

Could seasonal celebrations strengthen your neighborhood's identity and help focus activity?

Could programs be developed around the social history and ethnic cultures of the surrounding neighborhood?

CHANGES IN PARK ELEMENTS

Can plantings, fountains, and water systems be chosen to enhance seasonal changes?

How might these natural elements signal the seasonal passage of time?

TIME-SHARING SPACE

Could pedestrians and vehicles use the same space at different times, on different days, or in different seasons?

Would lighting or other systems have to be changed to permit this kind of time-sharing?

MOVEMENT: *RECREATION*

Recreation refreshes strength and spirit. Our parks and public gardens are a sign of the city's commitment to the re-creation of the community's life. Residents move out of their private homes and gardens to connect with the greater community in the public garden. Without free and convenient access to natural elements, such as lakes, creeks, fields, and the Mississippi River, city dwellers are impoverished—at least in spirit. No sculpted waterfall, planter, or shopping mall can replace the public garden in this respect.

ACCESSIBILITY

Does public space lie within a five-minute walk from your home and garden?

Is most of the public garden bordered by roadways ? How does the nearness of streets affect the sense of safety and security in the park?

Are gardens, paths, playing fields, and buildings barrier-free for all residents?

GATHERING

Is the public garden a natural gathering point for your neighborhood? Why?

Does the garden encourage informal meetings among neighbors and between neighbohoods?

Which recreational features draw people to the garden? How do people interact?

Does the space allow people to comfortably choose their activities—to join groups or to be left alone?

CONNECTING

Are city bike trails and walkways connected with your public garden?

Could stairs, ramps, bridges, and other structures connect topographic and built spaces to enhance the overall experience of the space?

Can people reach the garden conveniently by public transit?

Does the garden connect to larger systems of open space?

F. W. WOOLWORTH CO.

SLATED FOR DEMO
BROADWAY

PENN/BROADWAY —
COMPLICATED
STREETS.
LIQUOR STORE
CONTROVERSY.

LOTS OF
PEDESTRIANS.

MIX OF NEIGHBORHOOD
BUSINESSES,
CHURCHES &
BURGER KING

HISTORIC
MARKS

ST. ANN
AN-IMPE
NEIGHBO
LOCATED

STOREFR

PEDESTRIAN PROPORTION

PEDESTRIAN PROPORTION

EMPTY
STORES

ASHMARKET

ETHNIC
BUSINESSES

PENN
POLIC
IS A
COMM

VARIETY SHOPS

LOCAL MENU

ORGANIZING
WHAT YOU'VE DISCOVERED

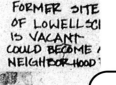

A NEIGHBORHOOD IS A COMPLEX SYSTEM. AS WITH ANY SYSTEM, WE CAN BEGIN TO DECIPHER ITS WORKINGS USING SOME GENERAL PRINCIPLES.

It's tempting to start planning with a clean sheet of paper and its logical extension, the empty block. But in reality, each neighborhood is a messy amalgam of the natural and the built, the moving and the fixed, the evolving and the permanent. Moreover, these intricate layers and shifting networks are the foundation for a vital, interesting community. So before reaching for an eraser—or a bulldozer— here are some suggestions for making sense of what's already there.

We recommend that you begin by analyzing the physical features of your neighborhood. For starters, use the themes outlined in the previous chapters. Take this book with you on field trips and to resident meetings. Alone or with a group, answer the chapter questions with a combination of photographs, diagrams, and words. Encourage participants to jot down questions, draw on maps, or scribble notes on photos. Remember, in this note-taking exercise, neatness doesn't matter.

As a next step, we found it helpful to organize our responses in a matrix. This gridded cross-referencing arrangement can reveal how physical features relate to the life of your neighborhood. As the headings for the columns in our matrix, we listed the five physical features outlined in this book—Homes and Gardens, Community Streets, Neighborhood Niche, Anchoring Institutions and Public Gardens. The five organizational themes—Location, Scale, Mix, Time and Movement— became headings for the rows. Be prepared: Your matrix will grow as participants add their words and pictures, so set aside a large wall in your work space for this preplanning exercise.

Constructing a matrix as a group planning exercise or sharing the results of individual matrices can help you and your neighbors better understand your community and how to shape its future. By inviting many points of view, the process helps participants see their neighborhood through new eyes. By focusing on areas to be preserved or improved, you can frame questions for further discussion. And together you can discover a set of common values to guide future change.

The neat categories we developed while looking at many city neighborhoods may not fit yours. You may decide that other categories or themes are more pertinent to your neighborhood. Or you may decide to use another organizing scheme entirely. Whatever the means, the goal is the same: to explore and refine your vision of a richer, more habitable community landscape.

Analyzing even the smallest neighborhood can seem like a job of overwhelming complexity. Decide on ways to break the task down into more manageable parts. For example, perhaps

VARIETY & RANGE

ORGANIZING THEMES

INDIVIDUAL YARDS

SMALL, MID-BLOC

LOCATION: on common ground

PLANTS IN THE YARD → PLEASANT FOR PEOPLE WALKING BY...

PRIVATE FLOWER GARDENS – BUT NO COMMUNITY GARDENS.

COTTAGE PA 'WEDGE' PARK IRREGULAR S PATTERN – TOPOGRAPHIC R RESPONSE.

SCALE: visually accessible

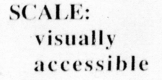

Cottage Park play area — visible from home

MIX: compatible activities

FOREST HEIGHTS CHURCH

using disposable wide-angle cameras, you and your neighbors can photograph the assets, problems and opportunities in your community, as in the photos below of a Twin Cities neighborhood. Before you set out, agree on a theme to investigate as a group. For example, what are the features that make your neighborhood safe, interesting, or inviting to pedestrians? Discussing these photos in thematic clusters is one way to explore your values and perceptions together.

Or consider appointing subcommittees to study individual neighborhood features. Encourage participants to ask questions and jot down observations in a variety of formats. The matrix below uses photos, maps, drawings, and words to analyze the "public gardens" of the Jordan neighborhood. In this exercise, the group looked at all types of public gardens, including yards, play areas, neighborhood parks, greenways, and regional parks.

DEVELOPING A MATRIX OR A FRAMEWORK IS IMPORTANT:

AS AN ORGANIZING TOOL Frameworks can help you to better understand your community by breaking its overwhelming complexity into simpler parts.

AS A DISCUSSION TOOL Frameworks can help organize participants' notes and focus group discussions while revealing the diversity of neighborhood values and perceptions.

After subcommittees have studied the individual physical features of the neighborhood, the neighborhood can work together to prepare a summary matrix that illustrates and describes all five physical features and their organizing themes. The matrix illustrated below covered the wall of a meeting room and was used to collect and organize information about one Twin Cities neighborhood.

Working within a framework will help you to see the pieces of your community, their relationships, and how they add up to form a unique whole. It will help make the physical environment visible so you can more clearly see areas of common ground with your neighbors, as well as the differences within your shared environment. The examples presented here do not contain the "right" answers. They may not even contain the right categories. But they offer a vocabulary and means for starting your discovery process.

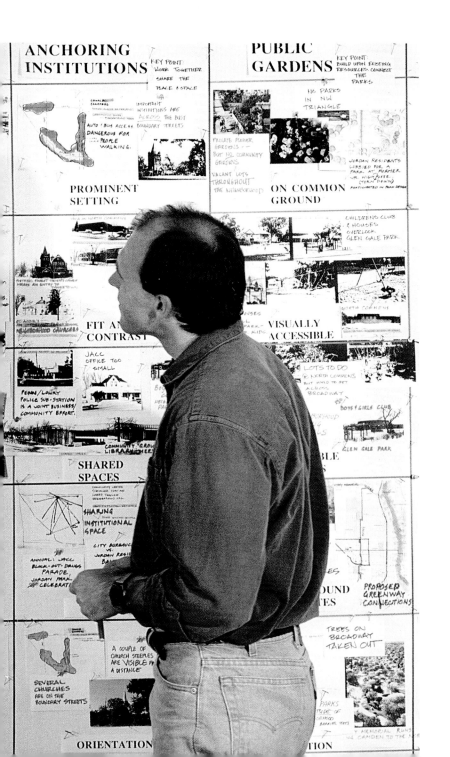

Six Planning Steps

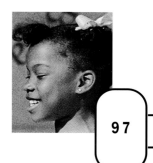

FOR NEIGHBORHOODS THAT ARE READY TO START PLANNING, THIS SIX-STEP PROCESS WILL ALLOW YOU TO INCORPORATE THE URBAN DESIGN CONCEPTS PRESENTED IN THE EARLIER CHAPTERS.

Our planning method is based upon asking six fundamental questions that will lead you through a process of discovery. The questions are: Can we agree to meet and work together for a common purpose? What kind of neighborhood do we have? What kind of neighborhood do we want? What kind of neighborhood can we make? How do we put the plan to work in our neighborhood? What do we need to sustain our neighborhood?

The process is more of a road map than a cookbook. It provides a framework for the activities your neighborhood may decide to undertake. But the individual steps should be modified as required to meet the specific needs of your neighborhood.

Although the six steps are presented here as a sequence, they are not always separate events with clear beginnings and endings. In fact, steps may overlap. Remember, planning is a continuous process that grows richer and deeper over time. For example, "Sustaining" is not the final step, but a continuation and enrichment of the others. Each pass through the process builds broader citizen participation, closer community ties, a clearer sense of purpose, and stronger neighborhood organizations and institutions.

View the process as building the neighborhood rather than making a neighborhood plan. Then it becomes clear that your product will be a continually self-revitalizing neighborhood, not a fat planning document.

STEP 1. ORGANIZING

CAN WE AGREE TO MEET AND WORK TOGETHER FOR A COMMON PURPOSE?

Neighborhoods often decide to organize only when confronted with a problem that makes enough residents worried or mad. Once they start meeting for one reason, however, they often find that they have common interests that go beyond the specific issue. Ideally, a neighborhood should ask this question first, before unwelcome change begins to control the agenda that brings them together. Instead of focusing on narrow (and often negative) concerns, they can start with the broader, positive attributes of the neighborhood that can form a basis for an overall neighborhood plan.

WHAT YOU'LL DO To initiate a neighborhood plan, residents need to form a group to lead the planning efforts. This planning group should have broad representation from neighborhood organizations, local institutions, the local business community, and interested neighborhood residents at large. Each neighborhood can choose how to mix these constituent groups in a way that best represents the general characteristics of their neighborhood.

Many neighborhoods already have individuals and groups that are accomplished organizers. But remember that this form of organizing is broader and more inclusive than traditional political and single-issue organizing. Some people who should be members of this group might not see eye-to-eye if organized around single issues. There might even be some valuable contributors who might never before have signed up for a "planning group." Before focusing on issues:

> Agree to meet and work together for a common purpose.
>
> Create a planning group with broad representation.
>
> Discuss everyone's goals and objectives, beliefs, and assumptions, to create a common vocabulary and to form a common basis for planning.

WHAT YOU'LL DISCOVER Organizing is the first step, but it never really stops. It takes time to build a neighborhood planning organization, educate the community about your activities, and gather support for your efforts. Steps 2 through 5 will provide needed information and establish vital community connections that will strengthen and sustain your organizational efforts over time.

WHAT YOU'LL PRODUCE/CREATE The most important result of effective organizing is a strong neighborhood coalition that sees the neighborhood planning process as an important source of community knowledge and strength. Because the process is fun and enlightening—and not just about political power—a broad range of people will emerge to participate and carry ideas into reality.

SOME SUGGESTIONS

Find a place to meet and work where you can leave maps and drawings over the long term.

Develop ground rules for how the planning group intends to work together.

Create a work plan that outlines the general planning process and initial steps that you intend to follow in your neighborhood. Don't concentrate on the most pressing problem.

Work on defining physical, social, and economic issues simultaneously.

Keep documents that record your initial purposes for meeting and working together.

Look at areas of unrealized opportunity to improve your neighborhood.

Agree to meet together and work for a common purpose.

STEP 2. GATHERING

WHAT KIND OF NEIGHBORHOOD DO WE HAVE?

The previous sections of this book dealt with learning to see Twin Cities neighborhoods in terms of physical features and organizing themes. This step allows you to apply some of those ideas. Gathering is the search for those positive physical features that will become the basis for building or improving your neighborhood. The information you gather about your neighborhood resources will help you better identify its needs and opportunities. Gathering can also help you create a common ground for exchange between your neighborhood and the city.

WHAT YOU'LL DO The gathering process consists of three major parts—"Reviewing," "Looking Around" (see also "What You'll Discover," opposite), and "Asking Around."

Reviewing A great deal of information about your neighborhood already exists. It isn't necessarily collected in a form that makes it immediately useful. This information includes base maps, demographic statistics, and other data used by the city planners. In its raw form, it may lack sufficient block-by-block detail or require interpretation, but it provides a good place to start. Historical documents, including old plans, streetcar and road maps, photos or early resident accounts, may be discovered in library history collections or public archives. Long-time residents or family-owned businesses are often excellent resources for neighborhood stories and history.

Looking Around This part of the process is neither superficial sightseeing nor cold inventorying of trees and fire hydrants. It allows you to become a student of your own community, intent upon understanding—and appreciating—what already shapes the neighborhood's character. The framework in the earlier chapters summarizes the relationship between the five physical features and five organizing themes. The framework, and the categories it contains, provides a useful common vocabulary for discussing and defining neighborhood design issues. It can provide collection baskets to help you identify the information you need to gather.

In addition to the investigation by the planning group using city-generated base maps and data, you may decide to:
Plan a walking tour that asks neighbors to look at and record neighborhood resources.
Get your planning group and neighborhood residents together for a bus tour of other neighborhoods that might illustrate useful examples.

Asking Around As you prepare to initiate a neighborhood plan, it is important to find out what what people outside the planning group think. You may decide to construct a questionnaire to identify key issues and underlying attitudes of the neighborhood about the nature and quality of the physical environment. Also be sure to find out what public and private interests are already planning—and how the community might participate. Here's a sampling of places to ask around about plans that can have an impact on your neighborhood.

For information about your neighborhood, contact:

City planning department—for current planning and zoning issues

City manager, mayor, city council, and/or county board—for capital improvements planned for your neighborhood and other neighborhoods in your city

Economic development or redevelopment authority—for their responsibilities for expanding the economic vitality of your community

Public works department—for infrastructure improvements (streets, sewers, lights, etc.) being planned in your neighborhood

Local business associations, developers, and nonprofit organizations—for improvement or expansion projects being planned for your neighborhood

Parks and recreation department, and school board—for planned changes in programming

WHAT YOU'LL DISCOVER Through this gathering process, you'll begin to see your neighborhood in new ways. You will unearth layers of history, discover new resources and identify new connections among the familiar features of your neighborhood. You'll also forge or strengthen ties with public agencies. And you'll likely have to reassess your ideas, beliefs, and assumptions about your neighborhood. Out of the discoveries about physical relationships will emerge economic and social questions. Why do residents shop primarily in this area instead of another commercial zone that is no farther away? Why do homes on this street seem more rundown than homes in the next block? Gathering what you have leads naturally to the next question: "What do we want?"

WHAT YOU'LL PRODUCE/CREATE The maps and documents that evolve out of this step will capture your newfound awareness and insights into the neighborhood.

A book of basic neighborhood facts that incorporates information from the city resources and your own gathering process.

A collection of contemporary (and perhaps historic) photographs from your neighborhood and other areas showing features you like.

A resource map that locates and identifies key resources and unique features.

A neighborhood inventory that analyzes the physical features of your neighborhood.

SOME SUGGESTIONS

Ask residents from other neighborhoods what makes your neighborhood unique.

Look at other neighborhoods as well as your own to see what makes them unique. Often it is easier initially to see the resources others have than to identify your own.

Neighborhoods have perceived as well as political boundaries. Be sure to include resources that you share with adjacent neighborhoods, even if they are outside the "official" boundaries of your area.

STEP 3. ORDERING

WHAT KIND OF NEIGHBORHOOD DO WE WANT?

In the ordering process, you begin to reach important agreements that will form the base of the neighborhood plan. You will then express them in a mission statement that defines a future image for your neighborhood. Finally, you will support the broader statement with long-range goals and clear, achievable objectives.

The information gathered in Step 2 can be ordered in a variety of ways. Explore as many directions as you can. By proposing and testing alternative scenarios, you'll establish the widest possible range of options that could be accommodated within your vision for the neighborhood. Then you can narrow the alternatives to one scenario that attracts a clear consensus.

WHAT YOU'LL DO In Step 2, you set out to collect information about neighborhood resources in physical categories. But in looking at the products from Step 2, you will likely find a variety of physical/environmental, social, and economic issues spilling out of the original categories. Step 3 allows you to redraw the physical picture of the neighborhood, while beginning to evaluate these issues. To answer the larger question about the kind of neighborhood you want, the group must answer a series of questions raised by the information gathered in Step 2: Where are we now? Which ways can we go? Which way is best?

WHERE ARE WE NOW? To start, your neighborhood planning group must agree on the information about needs and resources that has been gathered. Is the information correct? Is there enough on each subject to be useful? Does everyone make similar assumptions about this information, or do you have different ways of interpreting the same data?

WHICH WAYS CAN WE GO? The task of evaluating the alternative directions suggested by all this information can seem overwhelming. One useful way to narrow down the range of options is to explore three general scenarios:

> Conserve: What can we do with a minimum amount of change?
>
> Revitalize: What can we do if we continue more of the same but do it better than we have in the past?
>
> Redevelop: What can we do with radical change?

Assign the scenarios to different work groups. Ask each group to describe and support a vision for the neighborhood, using the information on issues, needs, and opportunities as a base. For their scenario, each group should:

> Generate an outline of social, economic, and physical issues they discover.
>
> Hypothesize how their scenario might be implemented, identifying short- and long-term steps necessary to carry out their vision.
>
> Establish pros and cons for their scenario.

WHICH WAY IS BEST? Gather the entire group to evaluate the scenarios. Some new combination of issues will emerge from the different scenarios, and a more comprehensive vision plan can be built that better matches needs with resources.

WHAT YOU'LL DISCOVER After completing this step in the process, your neighborhood should be fully prepared to engage in the evaluation of plans, projects, and programs proposed. You'll have a clear understanding of what the community stands to lose or gain from each proposal. Equally important, you'll have an effective means to communicate this knowledge to others. Your resource assessment and preliminary vision plan will help you negotiate trade-offs and mitigate the impact of other projects.

WHAT YOU'LL PRODUCE/CREATE

A mission statement (a statement of purpose) for your neighborhood planning program.

A list of the physical, social, and economic needs.

A map that shows opportunities for improving or enhancing the physical environment.

A preliminary vision plan that summarizes your neighborhood's goals and prioritizes needs and available resources.

SOME SUGGESTIONS Use the framework of physical features and organizing themes to generate and identify specific opportunities and design questions.

Group the set of needs and opportunities into themes suggested by your work. For example, one neighborhood might focus on environment, housing quality, family and community unity, and businesses and institutions serving local residents. Another might identify crime, housing mix, job creation and community schools.

Step 4. Making

WHAT KIND OF NEIGHBORHOOD CAN WE MAKE?

In this step, you will field-test and refine your plan with the public and private sectors. You will show your plan to government officials, adjacent neighborhoods, and local nonprofit organizations. By sharing the plan, you can secure tacit approval from local units of government and governmental agencies. And, just as important, showcasing your plan allows others to comment on its merits and drawbacks before you carry it out.

Through this step in the process, the influence of your plan reaches beyond your neighborhood. Public officials begin to incorporate your goals and objectives into their political and public policy agendas. Public agencies must consider and comment on how their current plans fit with yours. Adjacent neighborhoods have the opportunity to point out areas of conflict with their plans. And you have the chance to incorporate some new ideas and considerations into your plan. You will have identified potential allies, barriers, and stumbling blocks. At the end of this step, your plan will have a strong mission statement, a set of goals and objectives, and a list of potential projects, policies and programs necessary to implement the plan.

WHAT YOU'LL DO Field-test your ideas by showing your vision plan and mission statement to as many elected and appointed officials, adjacent neighborhood groups, business groups, potential investors and grant agencies, and local nonprofit organizations as you can. Convey the plan as far and in as many directions as possible. Remember that the purpose of this step is to test the plan, not to sell it. Be prepared to collect opinions and information as you take the plan to the various constituencies.

104

As you test your ideas:

Ask the outside interests for their opinions about the feasibility of your vision plan.

Find out how your plan fits with any plans they might have.

As constraints arise in these discussions, work them into the discussion the next time you present the plan to others. Get other opinions to see if they are real concerns that should be incorporated into your revised plan.

Reality-test your assumptions by gathering additional information or by trying to look at the same pattern of facts from a different perspective. (For example, ask members of the group to role-play the part of the public works department, a developer, or a city council member.)

Check with other neighborhood organizations that have done similar things to see if they can provide you with information or technical assistance.

Identify existing projects, public policies, and programs that might assist you in implementing your plan.

Identify potential partners who can collaborate with your neighborhood organization on developing new projects, creating policies, or initiating programs.

WHAT YOU'LL DISCOVER These discussions will help you find potential partners who can contribute to the implementation of your plan. These partners may come from the business community, a government agency, or a nonprofit organization. Since most projects and programs will usually require some form of collaboration among these three sectors, identifying partners early on will enable you to include some of their needs and concerns in your plan.

This is the development phase. Be flexible and listen to the ideas and concerns of other individuals and organizations. As you encourage constructive dialogue about your plan with your neighbors and the larger community, you will see a more comprehensive and refined plan emerge.

WHAT YOU'LL PRODUCE/CREATE Most of the documents produced during this stage will be refinements of earlier work, including:

A reformulated vision plan and mission statement, which accommodates new information and new perspectives gained in your field-testing.

A list of potential projects necessary to implement the plan.

A preliminary outline of policies and programs that could help you implement your plan.

A framework to help you evaluate projects and programs proposed by others for your neighborhood.

SOME SUGGESTIONS

Potential partners can come from anywhere. Look for them in other neighborhood organizations, area corporations, nonprofit organizations, and all levels of government and civic institutions.

Packaging your vision plan into potential projects, policies, and programs may require technical assistance from a range of professionals, including architects, attorneys, bankers, and planners.

STEP 5. TAKING ACTION

HOW DO WE PUT THE PLAN TO WORK IN OUR NEIGHBORHOOD?

This step sets priorities for actions and activities, projects, and programs. You will need to reach a consensus about what things you want to do first and what resources you are willing to commit to accomplish these objectives.

The prioritizing process leads to the formulation of a comprehensive action plan. The action plan outlines each project, program, and policy necessary. It outlines the agreements and accommodations that must be negotiated with the public, private, and nonprofit sectors. And it identifies the resources you'll need and where to get them.

WHAT YOU'LL DO

Meet and discuss with your neighbors to establish an action program based on your vision plan, goals, and objectives.

Gather broad community support for your plan and action program by meeting with public officials, nonprofit organizations, and members of the private sector.

Assign responsibilities for tasks to individuals or groups.

Make agreements, arrangements, and accommodations, including investment strategies, that the neighborhood and other sectors will support over time.

106

WHAT YOU'LL DISCOVER During the earlier steps of the planning process, you have gradually been moving your chair closer to the table where the decisions that affect your neighborhood get made. In forging a realistic plan, you have also gathered the necessary community support and built a strong planning organization, which allows you to negotiate for what you want—rather than fight for it.

The old pattern, in which the public sector assumes responsibility for dealing with developers on behalf of neighborhoods, sometimes works. But other times it results in inappropriate projects that spark neighborhood resistance, which becomes costly for the developers who must rework proposals and cope with delays.

A comprehensive framework actually makes it easier for public agencies and private developers to work with your neighborhood. Developers then have better information upon which to base their plans to suit local needs, and public agencies spend less time refereeing disputes.

WHAT YOU'LL PRODUCE/CREATE

An action program that establishes priorities, sets clear strategies, and outlines tasks for specific actions or activities needed to implement the plan.

Agreements for multisector collaborations to initiate needed programs and accomplish specific projects.

Support for the planning group to negotiate on behalf of the neighborhood.

SOME SUGGESTIONS

Seek out professional organizations, such as the American Institute of Architects and the American Planning Association, that can provide you with information or technical assistance to formulate plans and programs.

Elect or help appoint public officials who will institute public policies that support your plan.

State measurable actions or activities that will help you track your progress.

Step 6. Sustaining

WHAT DO WE NEED TO SUSTAIN OUR NEIGHBORHOOD?

A neighborhood, like any other structure, requires a constant cycle of maintenance and management. A neighborhood stays built best when a recognized organization assumes ongoing responsibility for it. Whatever means of administration and management you establish, it must be supported fully by the entire neighborhood. And the neighborhood organization must be recognized within the larger community as a legitimate negotiating instrument for the neighborhood.

WHAT YOU'LL DO

Establish a means to administer and monitor projects and programs.

Continue to plan and negotiate projects, programs, and policies that will improve your neighborhood. Periodically re-evaluate Steps 1 through 5, asking:

> Do we represent the neighborhood? Has the makeup of the neighborhood changed since we developed our plan?

> Do we have the right information? What developments might have made our initial information gathering out-of-date?

> Do we need to re-examine our vision? What have we learned that is worth adding?

> Do we need to renegotiate our agreements, arrangements, and accommodations? Are the players in other sectors different from the ones we first dealt with? Have political or economic conditions changed?

> Are we taking appropriate actions? Are they having the desired effects? How do we measure our progress?

> Are we involved enough to sustain our neighborhood? Do we need new blood or new challenges?

> Do we need to look for new financial collaborators, partners, or grants as support runs out? Have we found ways to make our efforts financially self-sustaining?

WHAT YOU'LL DISCOVER

For the neighborhood building process to sustain itself, the organization must be part cop and part cheerleader. As a cop, it must monitor projects and programs to ensure that all parties are honoring their agreements. As a cheerleader, it must keep people informed and involved. Good monitoring of agreements sets up the proper expectations on the part of the collaborators. A community education program will help your neighborhood make better plans and more effectively evaluate the proposals from others.

WHAT YOU'LL PRODUCE/CREATE

A community education program that informs residents about the plan and planning program for the neighborhood.

A means for inviting and integrating new, committed members as others leave.

SOME SUGGESTIONS

By involving local school children in your community education program, you will also reach a number of parents in your neighborhood who might not otherwise participate in neighborhood planning.

Share risks, responsibilities, and rewards with multisector collaborators.

STEP 1. ORGANIZING

CAN WE AGREE TO MEET AND WORK TOGETHER FOR A COMMON PURPOSE?

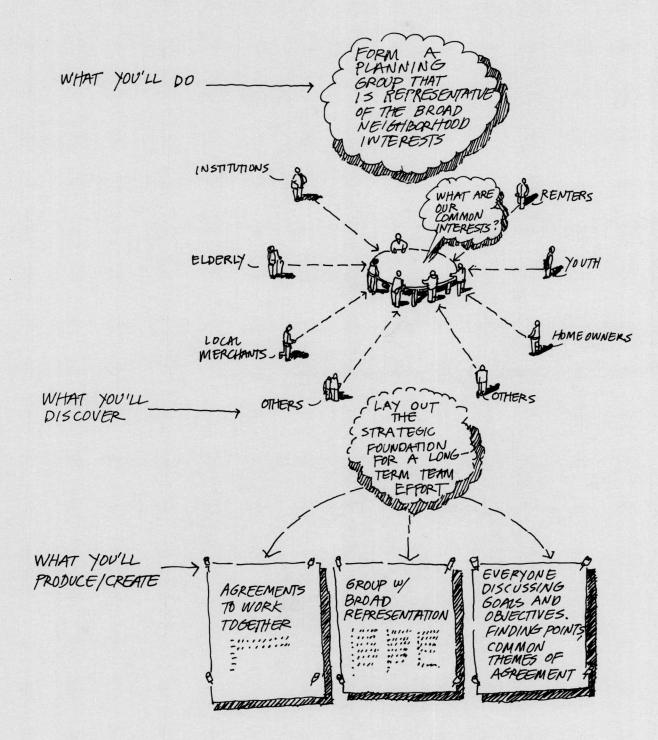

WHAT YOU'LL DO → FORM A PLANNING GROUP THAT IS REPRESENTATIVE OF THE BROAD NEIGHBORHOOD INTERESTS

INSTITUTIONS

WHAT ARE OUR COMMON INTERESTS?

RENTERS

ELDERLY

YOUTH

LOCAL MERCHANTS

HOME OWNERS

WHAT YOU'LL DISCOVER → OTHERS

LAY OUT THE STRATEGIC FOUNDATION FOR A LONG-TERM TEAM EFFORT

OTHERS

WHAT YOU'LL PRODUCE/CREATE →

AGREEMENTS TO WORK TOGETHER

GROUP W/ BROAD REPRESENTATION

EVERYONE DISCUSSING GOALS AND OBJECTIVES. FINDING POINTS, COMMON THEMES OF AGREEMENT

111

STEP 2. GATHERING
WHAT KIND OF NEIGHBORHOOD DO WE HAVE?

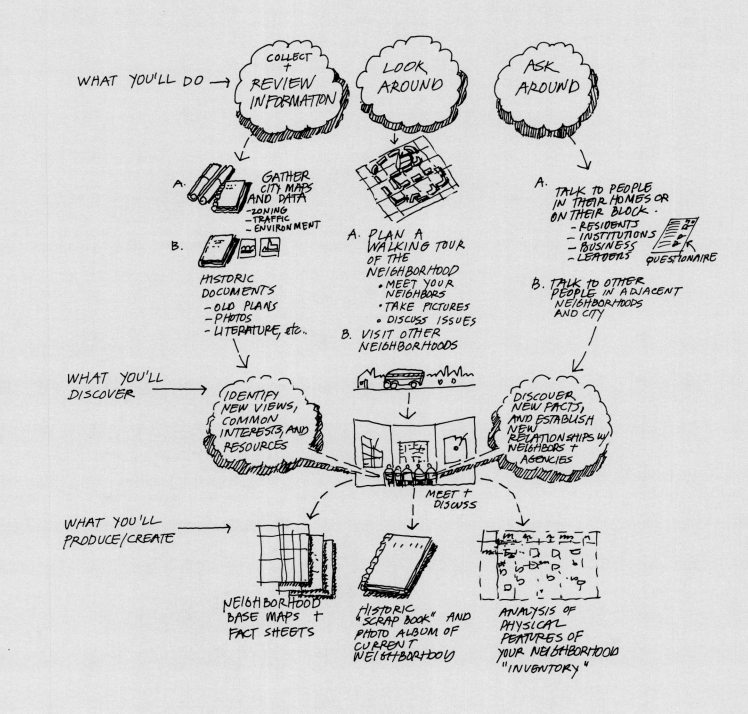

WHAT YOU'LL DO →

COLLECT + REVIEW INFORMATION

LOOK AROUND

ASK AROUND

A. GATHER CITY MAPS AND DATA
- ZONING
- TRAFFIC
- ENVIRONMENT

B. HISTORIC DOCUMENTS
- OLD PLANS
- PHOTOS
- LITERATURE, etc.

A. PLAN A WALKING TOUR OF THE NEIGHBORHOOD
- MEET YOUR NEIGHBORS
- TAKE PICTURES
- DISCUSS ISSUES

B. VISIT OTHER NEIGHBORHOODS

A. TALK TO PEOPLE IN THEIR HOMES OR ON THEIR BLOCK.
- RESIDENTS
- INSTITUTIONS
- BUSINESS
- LEADERS

QUESTIONNAIRE

B. TALK TO OTHER PEOPLE IN ADJACENT NEIGHBORHOODS AND CITY

WHAT YOU'LL DISCOVER →

IDENTIFY NEW VIEWS, COMMON INTERESTS, AND RESOURCES

DISCOVER NEW FACTS, AND ESTABLISH NEW RELATIONSHIPS W/ NEIGHBORS + AGENCIES

MEET + DISCUSS

WHAT YOU'LL PRODUCE/CREATE →

NEIGHBORHOOD BASE MAPS + FACT SHEETS

HISTORIC "SCRAP BOOK" AND PHOTO ALBUM OF CURRENT NEIGHBORHOOD

ANALYSIS OF PHYSICAL FEATURES OF YOUR NEIGHBORHOOD "INVENTORY"

Step 3. Ordering
What Kind of Neighborhood Do We Want?

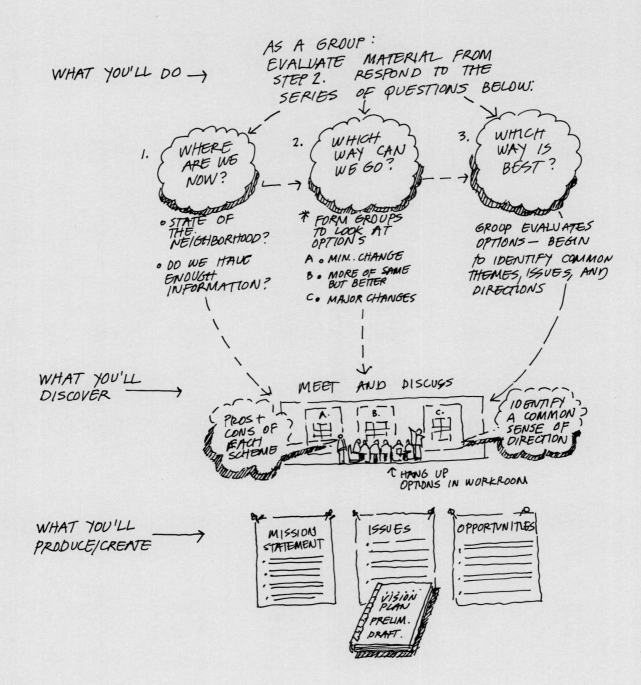

WHAT YOU'LL DO →

AS A GROUP:
EVALUATE MATERIAL FROM STEP 2. RESPOND TO THE SERIES OF QUESTIONS BELOW:

1. WHERE ARE WE NOW?
   - STATE OF THE NEIGHBORHOOD?
   - DO WE HAVE ENOUGH INFORMATION?

2. WHICH WAY CAN WE GO?
   * FORM GROUPS TO LOOK AT OPTIONS
   A • MIN. CHANGE
   B • MORE OF SAME BUT BETTER
   C • MAJOR CHANGES

3. WHICH WAY IS BEST?
   GROUP EVALUATES OPTIONS — BEGIN to IDENTIFY COMMON THEMES, ISSUES, AND DIRECTIONS

WHAT YOU'LL DISCOVER →

MEET AND DISCUSS

PROS + CONS OF EACH SCHEME

A. B. C.

↑ HANG UP OPTIONS IN WORKROOM

IDENTIFY A COMMON SENSE OF DIRECTION

WHAT YOU'LL PRODUCE/CREATE →

MISSION STATEMENT

ISSUES

OPPORTUNITIES

VISION PLAN PRELIM. DRAFT.

WHAT KIND OF NEIGHBORHOOD CAN WE MAKE?

114

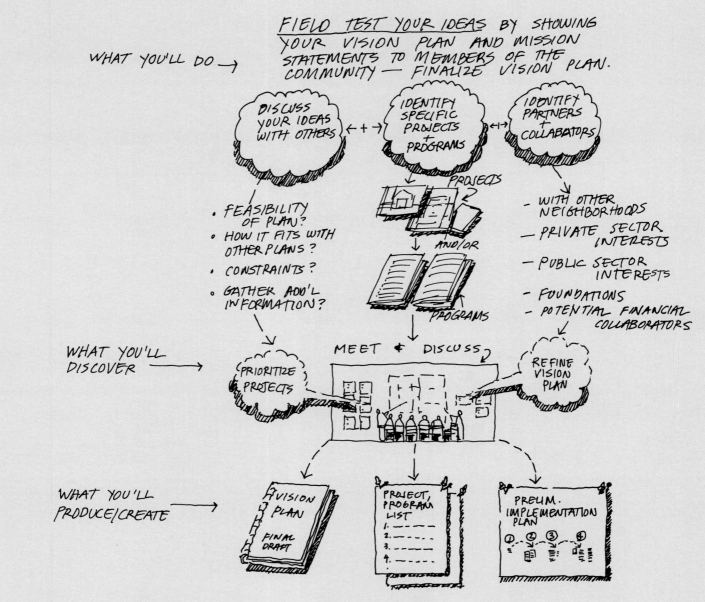

WHAT YOU'LL DO →

FIELD TEST YOUR IDEAS BY SHOWING YOUR VISION PLAN AND MISSION STATEMENTS TO MEMBERS OF THE COMMUNITY — FINALIZE VISION PLAN.

DISCUSS YOUR IDEAS WITH OTHERS

IDENTIFY SPECIFIC PROJECTS + PROGRAMS

IDENTIFY PARTNERS + COLLABORATORS

• FEASIBILITY OF PLAN?
• HOW IT FITS WITH OTHER PLANS?
• CONSTRAINTS?
• GATHER ADD'L INFORMATION?

PROJECTS

AND/OR

PROGRAMS

- WITH OTHER NEIGHBORHOODS
- PRIVATE SECTOR INTERESTS
- PUBLIC SECTOR INTERESTS
- FOUNDATIONS
- POTENTIAL FINANCIAL COLLABORATORS

WHAT YOU'LL DISCOVER →

PRIORITIZE PROJECTS

MEET & DISCUSS

REFINE VISION PLAN

WHAT YOU'LL PRODUCE/CREATE →

VISION PLAN FINAL DRAFT

PROJECT, PROGRAM LIST
1.
2.
3.
4.

PRELIM. IMPLEMENTATION PLAN

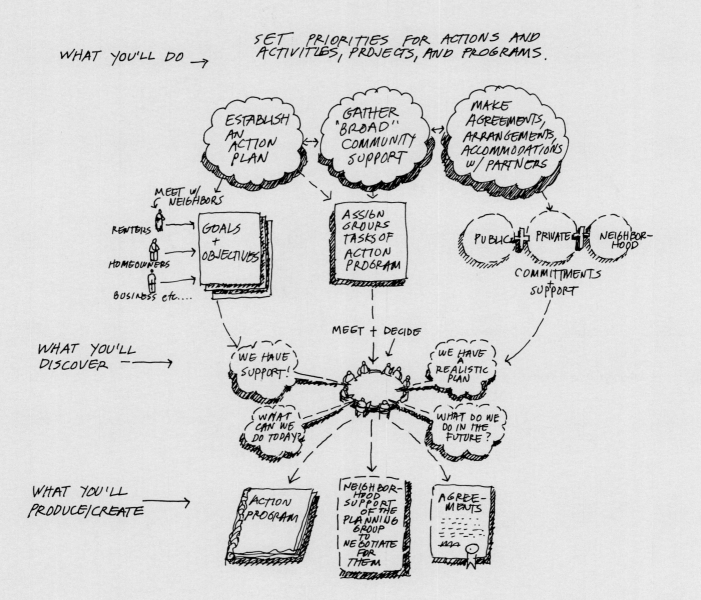

WHAT YOU'LL DO → SET PRIORITIES FOR ACTIONS AND ACTIVITIES, PROJECTS, AND PROGRAMS.

115

Step 6. Sustaining

WHAT DO WE NEED TO SUSTAIN OUR NEIGHBORHOOD?

WHAT YOU'LL DO → ESTABLISH AN ORGANIZATION FOR CONTINUAL MAINTENANCE AND MANAGEMENT OF NEIGHBORHOOD PROJECTS AND PROGRAMS.

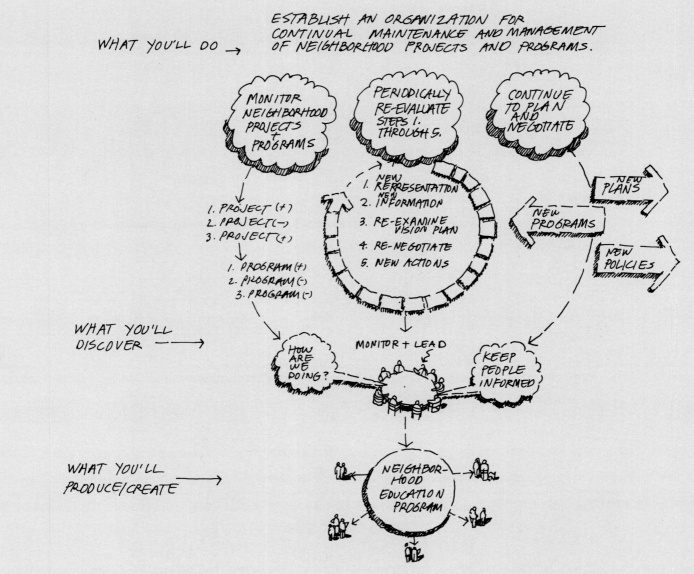

MONITOR NEIGHBORHOOD PROJECTS + PROGRAMS

PERIODICALLY RE-EVALUATE STEPS 1. THROUGH 5.

CONTINUE TO PLAN AND NEGOTIATE

1. PROJECT (+)
2. PROJECT (—)
3. PROJECT (+)

1. PROGRAM (+)
2. PROGRAM (—)
3. PROGRAM (—)

1. NEW REPRESENTATION
2. NEW INFORMATION
3. RE-EXAMINE VISION PLAN
4. RE-NEGOTIATE
5. NEW ACTIONS

NEW PLANS

NEW PROGRAMS

NEW POLICIES

WHAT YOU'LL DISCOVER — — →

HOW ARE WE DOING?

MONITOR + LEAD

KEEP PEOPLE INFORMED

WHAT YOU'LL PRODUCE/CREATE →

NEIGHBOR-HOOD EDUCATION PROGRAM

116

PHOTOGRAPHIC LOCATIONS AND CREDITS

All unattributed photos are by Design Center for
American Urban Landscape, University of Minnesota

Cover: Sunset Blvd., Cedar-Isles neighborhood, Minneapolis
2   Victory Memorial Pkwy. Minneapolis, Chris LaFontaine
8   Lake Nokomis neighborhood, Minneapolis
10   Minnehaha Creek, Hiawatha neighborhood, Minneapolis
12   Lake St. and Nicollet Ave., Minneapolis, Laurel Cazin
14   Aquatennial Parade, Minneapolis, Laurel Cazin
14   St. Alban's St. and Laurel Ave., St. Paul
16   St. Alban's Circle, St. Paul, Chris LaFontaine
18   Rose Fête, Minneapolis Institute of Art, Laurel Cazin
20   Linden Hills, Minneapolis, Vance Gellert
23   Minnehaha Creek, Minneapolis
24   Mounds Park, St. Paul, Laurel Cazin
25   Powderhorn Park, Minneapolis
      St. Paul, Laurel Cazin
26   Minneapolis, Laurel Cazin
28   Powderhorn Park neighborhood, Minneapolis
      Minneapolis, Laurel Cazin
30   Lake Nokomis neighborhood, Minneapolis
32   Milwaukee Ave., Minneapolis, Glenn Halvorson
34   Cathedral Hill neighborhood, St. Paul
35   Fair Oaks, Whittier neighborhood, Minneapolis
      Selby/Western area, St. Paul
36   Selby/Western area, St. Paul
37   Loring Park, Minneapolis
      Frogtown neighborhood, St. Paul
38   Crocus Hill neighborhood, St. Paul
39   25th St. and Hennepin Ave., Minneapolis
      Selby/Western area, St. Paul
      Penn Ave., Minneapolis, Susan Braun
40   Frogtown neighborhood, St. Paul
41   Fair Oaks, Whittier neighborhood, Minneapolis
      Northrup neighborhood, Minneapolis, Susan Braun
      Crocus Hill, St. Paul
42   Twin Cities Marathon, Jerry Stebbins
44   Lowry Hill neighborhood, Minneapolis
      Victory Memorial Pkwy., Minneapolis
45   Eastman Flats, Nicollet Island, Minneapolis
      St. Paul, Laurel Cazin
46   St. Paul, Laurel Cazin
47   Uptown, Carag neighborhood, Minneapolis
      West Broadway, Minneapolis
48   ECCO-Uptown neighborhood, Minneapolis
      Whittier neighborhood, Minneapolis, Laurel Cazin
49   St. Anthony Main, Minneapolis, Susan Braun
      Hennepin Ave. and Lake St., Uptown, Minneapolis
50   Loring Park neighborhood, Minneapolis
51   Harmon Place, Loring Park neighborhood, Minneapolis
      St. Anthony Main, Minneapolis, Susan Braun
52   Sunset Blvd., Cedar-Isles neighborhood, Minneapolis
53   St. Paul Sculpture Garden, Laurel Cazin
      Whittier neighborhood, Minneapolis, Laurel Cazin
      King's Highway, Minneapolis
54   Linden Hills neighborhood niche, Minneapolis
56   Victoria Crossing, St. Paul, Chris LaFontaine
      Loring Café, Minneapolis
      Broadway Ave., Minneapolis, Susan Braun
57   Linden Hills neighborhood niche, Minneapolis
58   St. Anthony Park neighborhood niche, St. Paul
59   St. Paul, Laurel Cazin
      Hennepin Ave., Minneapolis

60   Beltrami neighborhood, Minneapolis
      Delmonico's, Minneapolis
61   Uptown area, Minneapolis
      Whittier neighborhood, Minneapolis
62   Uptown Art Fair, Minneapolis, Susan Braun
63   Cinco de Mayo Parade, St. Paul, Laurel Cazin
      W. A. Frost, Cathedral Hill, St. Paul
      Victoria Crossing, Summit-Hill District, St. Paul
64   Uptown, Minneapolis
      Whittier neighborhood, Laurel Cazin
      Victoria Crossing, St. Paul, Chris LaFontaine
66   Lake of the Isles, Minneapolis, Jerry Stebbins
68   Carnegie Library, St. Anthony Park, St. Paul
      Fuller neighborhood, Minneapolis
      Pow-wow, Powderhorn Park, Minneapolis, Laurel Cazin
69   State Capitol and Prospect Park, St. Paul, Laurel Cazin
70   College of St. Thomas, St. Paul, Chris LaFontaine
71   St. Agnes Church, Frogtown, St. Paul, Chris LaFontaine
      Sculpture Garden, Minneapolis, Jerry Stebbins
72   Rose Fête, Minneapolis Institute of Art, Laurel Cazin
      Pow-wow, Powderhorn Park, Minneapolis, Laurel Cazin
73   Institute of Arts and College of Art and Design, Minneapolis
74   Whittier neighborhood, Minneapolis, Laurel Cazin
      Schmidt Brewery, St. Paul, Jerry Stebbins
75   Cinco de Mayo Parade, St. Paul, Laurel Cazin
      Ice Castle, St. Paul Winter Carnival, Jerry Stebbins
      Minnesota State Fairgrounds, St. Paul, Jerry Stebbins
76   Cathedral Hill and downtown St. Paul, Chris LaFontaine
      Minnehaha Falls, Hiawatha neighborhood, Minneapolis
      Prospect Park neighborhood, Minneapolis
77   St. Mary's Basilica, Minneapolis
78   Mississippi River, St. Paul and Minneapolis
80   Loring Park, Minneapolis
81   Minnehaha Creek at the Mississippi River, Minneapolis
      Como Park Conservatory, St. Paul, Chris LaFontaine
      Bassett Creek, Harrison neighborhood, Minneapolis
82   Irvine Park, West Seventh District, St. Paul, Chris LaFontaine
      Nicollet Island Park, Mississippi River, Minneapolis
83   Bryn Mawr neighborhood, Minneapolis, Julie Bargmann
      Fair Oaks Park, Minneapolis, Laurel Cazin
84   Sumner Glenwood neighborhood, Minneapolis,
      Star Tribune/Minneapolis-St. Paul
85   Bassett Creek, Minneapolis
      St. Paul, Laurel Cazin
86   Minnesota lake, Jerry Stebbins
87   Lake of the Isles, Minneapolis, Laurel Cazin
      Lake Harriet, Minneapolis
88   Irene Hixon Whitney Bridge, Minneapolis
      Lake Harriet, Minneapolis
89   Lake Calhoun, Minneapolis
      St. Paul Sculpture Garden, Laurel Cazin
90   Jordan neighborhood, Minneapolis, Susan Braun
92   Jordan neighborhood, Minneapolis, Susan Braun
94   Jordan neighborhood, Minneapolis, Susan Braun
96   Whittier neighborhood, Minneapolis, Laurel Cazin
99   Fair Oaks Park, Minneapolis, Laurel Cazin
      Whittier neighborhood, Minneapolis, Laurel Cazin
101 Whittier neighborhood, Minneapolis, Laurel Cazin
103 Whittier neighborhood festival, Minneapolis, Laurel Cazin
105 Minneapolis, Laurel Cazin
106 Pleasant Ave. Green Chair Project, Minneapolis, Joel Sisson
107 Pleasant Ave. Green Chair Project, Minneapolis, Joel Sisson
109 Jefferson Elementary School, Minneapolis, Vance Gellert

WE, THE CITIZENS, HAVE BE
LEGACY. THE GIFT OF OUR CI
BLOCK, LAYER BY LAYER, FO
YEARS BY THOSE WHO CAME
WARD FROM OUR DOWNTOWN
TAIN IT—ARE HOMES, INFRAST
DIVERSE SOCIAL FABRIC, WH
BUT WE RECOGNIZE THAT OUR
THEREFORE, WE DECLARE OUR
AND PLEDGE OUR EFFORTS
HOODS, STABLE SCHOOLS, AFF
STREETS, RESOURCEFUL DEVE
TO GOODS, SERVICES, AND J
THE NATURAL ENVIRONMENT.
THIS GIFT, BUT LEAVE IT GREA
TIFUL THAN IT WAS GIVEN TO
MON GROUND—IS A GOOD PLA

N GIVEN A GREAT PHYSICAL
Y HAS BEEN BUILT BLOCK BY
R MORE THAN ONE HUNDRED
BEFORE US. SPREADING OUT-
CORE—AND HELPING TO SUS-
UCTURES, SERVICES, AND THE
CH IS OUR COMMONWEALTH.
CITY IS AT A TURNING POINT.
STEWARDSHIP OF THIS LEGACY
O ENSURE SAFE NEIGHBOR-
ORDABLE HOUSING, AMENABLE
LOPMENT, EQUITABLE ACCESS
BS, AND AN INTEGRATION OF
LET OUR ACTS NOT DIMINISH
ER, BETTER, AND MORE BEAU-
US. THIS GROUND—OUR COM-
E TO START.

Designed by Kristen McDougall

Printed by Ambassador Press, Inc.,
Minneapolis, Minnesota, on Warren Lustro Dull.
Bound by Midwest Editions,
Minneapolis, Minnesota.

Composed in Bodyshop
(headings), Storefront (subheadings),
and Memphis light (text).
Bodyshop and Storefront were
designed for this publication by Alex Tylevich
The fonts reflect the vernacular typography
of street and commercial signage.

The authors gratefully acknowledge the individuals who so generously participated in a series of civic forums during the research phase of this project. Their ideas, criticisms, and insights greatly enriched our efforts.

James Alcott
Mary Anderson
Sharon Sayles Belton
Thomas Berg
Regina Bonsignore
Ollie Byrum
Jay Clark
Norm Coleman
Dan Cornejo
David Cox
Earl Craig
Tom Eggum
Adelheid Fischer
Elizabeth Fitzsimons

Don Fraser
Thomas Hammerberg
Ray Harris
Richard Heath
Peter Hutchinson
Jay Jensen
Kellie Jones
Richard Miller
Polly Munts
Kris Nelson
Polly Nyberg
Kathy O'Brien
Megan O'Hara
Michael O'Keefe

Christine Podas-Larson
Rip Rapson
Peggy Reichert
Brenda St. Germaine
Jim Scheibel
Richard Schunn
Joe Selvaggio
Janet Shapiro
Richard L. Straub
Carol Swenson
Mihailo Temali
Lucy Thompson
Mary Vogel
Thomas Welna